WHERE IS MY WANDERING BOY TONIGHT?

———— ● ————

BOOKS BY
DAVID WAGONER

———— ● ————

NOVELS

The Man in the Middle (1954)
Money Money Money (1955)
Rock (1958)
The Escape Artist (1965)
Baby, Come on Inside (1968)
Where Is My Wandering Boy Tonight? (1970)

POEMS

Dry Sun, Dry Wind (1953)
A Place to Stand (1958)
The Nesting Ground (1963)
Staying Alive (1966)
New and Selected Poems (1969)

D A V I D   W A G O N E R

•

Where Is My Wandering Boy Tonight?

•

F A R R A R ,   S T R A U S   &   G I R O U X

N E W   Y O R K

●

FOR PATT,
WITH LOVE

———— ● ————

"Fall off and stay a while."

—*Traditional Western greeting
to anyone on horseback*

WHERE IS MY WANDERING BOY TONIGHT?

1

———— • ————

The son of a judge is worse off than the son of a preacher, and I thought I was the living proof. I bet Fred Haskell, whose old man was one of them tall skinny undertaker-looking kind of preachers—which should of given him a head start on me—I bet Fred I was worse off than him, but right away I started losing because he couldn't scrape up even ten cents to match me, him not getting no allowance at all. Then just in time my old man stopped my allowance for what he called back talk (but wasn't no more'n just *talk*), so we was even again.

But we didn't seem to have no way to prove it on his side or mine, oncet and for all. His old man was always coming up with some new idea like scrubbing Fred with pumice and drenching him with a bucket of well water on Saturdays regular. Then at church the next day he'd be craning around at me (Fred always had to sit way up front, and his old man would of had him up with his nose to the altar if he could) and holding out his hand and making his mouth move like he was saying, "Ten cents!" But I held out on him, which wasn't no harder than holding out on the collection plate: a coin snapped on the bottom sounds just like one going inside. And besides, I was sitting there alone with the housekeeper which beat pumice any time.

And every time Fred's old man would think up something new to knock, squeeze, punch, scrape, or wrench the Devil out of him, my old man would do him near as good without no Bible to help, most of the time not even The Law. When he got to going, he didn't need man nor beast nor jurisprudence to help him be in the right. He was just naturally right, and if you didn't believe it, you'd best not let him find out. He could spot a disbeliever without even putting on his gold-rimmed specs, without even turning around, without even being in the same room.

And when it come to judgments and decrees and rules and trials for young men, the Judge didn't need no support from the outside, neither up in the skies nor underfoot. He just laid it out cold in front of you, and there it was. You could take it, but you couldn't leave it.

Anyway, neither me nor Fred ever collected that ten cents, though we both earned it plenty of times—me with the Home Harness Mender consisting of clamp, punch, awl, rivet set, thread, and ball of wax for fixing rotten harness when it should of been throwed out, and Fred sitting (sitting *still*) through more prayer meetings and sermons and socials than you'd think the brain of man could fit on a calendar.

Back in them days—in the 1890's—in Slope, Wyoming, they thought they was going to amount to something, being on the railroad and a junction at that, but it sort of went sour and ran downhill and frittered out, and you won't find it on most maps unless you look hard, and you can just barely find it if you go there in the flesh on a dim day. But back then, things was humming, and a judge had a good business. My old man didn't have the job of hanging nobody or sending nobody to the penitentiary—there's no money to speak of in that. (Wyoming didn't even *have* a penitentiary yet, though they was building one just for fun.) He handled all kind of lawsuits for our county, and just to put it in the practicalest way: the madder a couple of cattlemen or land-grabbers or railroads get with each other, the more money the judge is going to rake in. The lawyers make their share, but it's a lot easier to change your lawyer than change your judge, especially when he looks like my old man did then: big and silvery-haired and broad both front and sideways and well tamped down. He looked like he'd been built to last and not just slapped on and propped up for the Fourth of July.

So by the time he got to be up in his sixties, he'd put by a nest egg so big nobody could see it, not even me. I think my old man lived modest apurpose because he didn't want it jawed around he was rich. Most people expected judges to be rich, but that didn't cut no grease with my old man. He knew they was supposed to be honest, first off, so he was up-holding the dignity of The Law by living in our small house.

Without his black robe on, he had to uphold his dignity with a three-inch-wide black-leather belt near as big as a saddle girth and a brass buckle down at the foot of the slope with AJH-LLD on it the size of a brand: Andrew Jackson Holcomb, the first part meant, and the second part meant he was trained fair, square, and legal to practice law, though he didn't need no practice any more telling them lawyers when to speak up, shut up, stand up, or sit down.

I'm Junior, but I put in enough time fighting to get called Jackson, and I was seventeen years old the summer I'm going to tell about. My old man's first wife didn't have no kids, and Ma only had me, then croaked six months later, and I was raised up by a string of housekeepers, the latest one having been at the job three years, and her biggest disappointment in life was she couldn't run the jail instead.

He had my future all strung out and staked like a claim: I was going to Harvard Law School and learn how to be a judge the hard way (my old man never even saw a college far as I know, but he knew how to confound anybody who tried to pry into *that* matter). He wanted to get me enrolled but figured I didn't know enough Law, so when I'd of rather been soaking up sunshine or even a little history (I don't mind reading, it all depends what it is), he had me wedged into a corner of his office behind a stack of the dustiest, dullest lawbooks that ever had their backs sewed together and glued into cowhide. Far as I was concerned, they could of sewed the fronts together too.

2

—— • ——

Just to show you how judges' and preachers' sons get special treatment, early one afternoon that summer, when I was let loose for a bit, I went over to Fred's house to see if there was anything to eat, which there usually wasn't, but I figured I couldn't do no worse'n at home where the housekeeper was off at her sewing circle, leaving a little bread and hard cheese and a couple gingersnaps, and there was Fred hanging around his own kitchen door like a tramp, sniffing and fidgety.

"What's going on?" I says, but I already knew because I could smell the pie myself.

"Cherry pie," he says, sniffing some more and sticking his hands in his back pants pockets and scuffling.

"I ain't seen top nor bottom of a pie in a month," I says.

"The housekeeper don't believe in them." Then I remembered to stick him with it. "Sons of preachers get to eat good."

He flashed a look at me, his eyes hollow. "I ain't getting no dinner today because I got the Commandments wrong at breakfast," he says. "I forgot about graven images."

"Thing to do is go ahead and graven yourself one," I says. "Then you won't forget it."

But Fred didn't like that kind of talk, so he pretended he hadn't heard me. "Sometimes my ma'll give me something if *he* ain't around," he says. "But she just run off to the sewing circle."

"What do they do with all them circles once they get them sewed?" I says.

"I don't know," Fred says.

I took a deep sniff. "Where's *he* at?" I says.

"Calling on the sick," Fred says, sounding kind of sick his own self.

"What's he call them?" I says.

Fred looked all around, scairt. "You're going to get me switched, talking like that."

I snuck a look through the back door, and there was the pie in a tin pie plate on a shelf by the pantry, with wisps of steam rising up out of it. "Why don't you eat the pie?" I says.

Fred scowled at me like he hadn't been thinking about it. "Don't be crazy," he says.

"Maybe she left it for you and forgot to tell you because she was in a hurry," I says.

He looked hopeful for a second, then shook his head.

I don't know what got into me then besides being hungry, but I says, "Let's snitch it."

"What?" he says, holding still and looking shocked.

"It wouldn't be snitching anyway," I says. "It's your own

family pie, ain't it? Besides, I'd help you do it, so it wouldn't be *all* your fault."

He gulped a couple times, then says, "It's too hot to eat." I picked his cap off his head and ducked through the back door and slid the cap under the hot pie plate before he could stop me, and I was coming out before he even got all the way in. "They'll think some tramp done it," I says.

He skittered along beside me, glancing all around and looking like a thief and trying to shield the pie with his body, and he says, "Let's put it back."

But I was already past the first fences and into the back lane that led to another lane alongside our stable and house, and I says, "What if we get caught putting it back? You'd get all the blame and no pie."

He come along then and kept quiet, and we half run on tiptoe to our lane and through the back door into our kitchen where I figured we could use a couple spoons and not get our fingers burnt off. I set the pie plate down on the big wooden table, give Fred his cap back, and hunted up the spoons. Then we set down on the bench and pulled it in close and got our elbows up on the table and just looked at that juicy pie which had bubbly slits all over the brown top crust.

"How we going to dig it out?" Fred says.

"Maybe we better let it cool some more," I says, enjoying myself now and not too extra hungry no more with it setting right there in front of us.

"Ma always cuts it with a knife," Fred says.

So I got up and fetched a butcher knife from back of the breadbox and slapped it down on the table, and I says, "Here, you can do the honors," feeling like a host at a party —though I'd never had no party before but could imagine.

"You better do it," Fred says.

"No, you do it," I says.

"We could still put it back," he says, licking his lips.

And my old man walked in through the back door at a time of day he wasn't supposed to be anywhere near home but presiding over the pore souls and shysters in court. He had on his black suit which made him look bigger and worse and a green-striped fancy duck vest which led the way out to his belt buckle, and he was just about to take off his big gray hat when he seen us.

"Well, well, what have we here?" he says, putting his hat back on and looking at us froze in front of the pie.

I glanced at Fred, and he looked like somebody going to get hanged, so I knew we was in for it.

"I don't recollect any talk about pie," my old man says, just standing there but finally moving to the other side of the table and putting his hands on it and surveying the pie and us. "Whose pie is it?"

"Fred's," I says, and Fred's face turned the color of cherry juice.

My old man set himself down on the opposite bench, taking a long time to do it and getting everything arranged just so. He took off his hat and put it aside and made sure he had elbow room and give his silvery bush of hair a couple pats and then folded his big white hands in front of him. "And where did Fred·happen to get it?" he says.

"His ma give it to him," I says. "In case he got hungry."

My old man stared at Fred who looked like he wouldn't be talking till next month sometime, and he says, "Did she give it to you direct? By hand?"

"She wasn't home," I says.

There was a long quiet spell, then my old man says, "How much do you figure that pie's worth? What kind is it?"

"Cherry," I says.

"Counting the cherries and the time it took somebody to pick them and pit them and the sugar and the flour and the shortening and the baking powder and the kindling for the stove and the labor to roll it out and slap it together and wash the bowls and rolling pin afterwards?" he says. "Including the pie plate which has come along with it as part and parcel."

"I don't know," I says. "A dollar?"

"I hope you're right because in that case it wouldn't be a felony but a misdemeanor," my old man says, and Fred let out a groan.

"We didn't mean no harm," I says. "We was just hungry."

"I take the spoons as prima-facie evidence of intent to eat and thereby destroy all traces of the crime," he says.

"We couldn't of et the pie plate," I says.

"And furthermore," he says, raising his voice to full size, "I take the butcher knife to be prima-facie evidence of armed robbery. What do you say to that?"

"That there's *our* butcher knife," I says. "We didn't have it with us. We was just going to cut the—" I stopped myself short.

"Cut what?" my old man says, casual.

"We was going to cut a burr out of Fred's hair," I says, knowing there was usually at least a couple in it.

My old man looked disappointed, then he says, "Do you have any witnesses that saw you with the pie and without the butcher knife that can support your claim it wasn't armed robbery?"

"I ain't going to locate no witnesses for the prosecution," I says. "It can go find them its own self. We just walked the pie over here to cool it off."

My old man turned solid for a couple seconds, just staring at me, and then he says, "I don't know how you learnt to talk English so bad. It must be hard to learn it as bad as that. Can't you listen to me? Or your teachers?"

"I talk like people," I says.

"Well, they don't talk like that at Harvard," my old man says. "How am I supposed to get you in there?"

"I don't know," I says. "Maybe it'll rub off on me."

My old man stood up, almost knocking the bench over backwards, and he reached for the pie plate, burning his fingers and having to snap them back and forth and blow on them. "Bring that pie," he says, "and come with me," and he clapped his hat on and stalked out the door. I used Fred's cap on it again, and we both followed him along the lanes to Fred's house where he rapped on the back door.

I could of told him I knew a couple other ways to talk, including most of his way, but they didn't seem to fit my mouth right. For instance, how could I talk to Fred (which is where I got most of my talking done, not to old folks) and not use the same kind of words he did? It wouldn't be sensible.

Our luck had ran out for sure because instead of nobody or even Mrs. Haskell—who might of give the pie away to save commotion—Rev. Haskell come to the door in his shirtsleeves, wiping his hands on a piece of sugar sack, having finished off all the sick people that afternoon and washing his hands of them.

My old man led the way in, pointed to the table where I was supposed to set the pie (and I done so), and says, "Wait," and went into the parlor with Fred's old man while we stood in the kitchen, breathing our last.

"I wish I never seen that pie," Fred says.

"Well, say you didn't," I says.

He looked at me, then the pie, and says, "It's setting on my cap."

Which it was, so I plucked it out from under and give it to Fred who put it on and took it off again. We could hear them muttering in the other room, both with deep bass voices, and then Rev. Haskell entered the kitchen slow like he was following a coffin. He had his shiny crinkled black frock coat on now and looked open for business, stretching himself up tall so's he wouldn't be shorter'n me and Fred.

He stared down at the pie and says, "All right, I want the truth," like he expected the pie to open up and talk.

"Fred never once touched that pie," I says. "It was me."

Acting startled, Rev. Haskell glanced back at my old man who was hovering outside the doorway, then says, "This is no time for self-sacrifice or martyrdom, Junior. Save your hide for more important occasions."

"It's the truth," I says. "He never so much as laid a finger on it. Or under it neither."

Rev. Haskell narrowed his eyes like a cat going to sleep and says, "Just because Frederick is easily led is no excuse. There's plenty of room in Hell for weak accomplices."

"He wasn't no accomplice," I says. "He was just a witness."

"Leave him speak for himself," Rev. Haskell says, louder. "If he wants to be a witness, he's going to be one for Jesus Christ and nobody else."

"I done it," Fred says, looking at the floor. "I sinned again."

Before Rev. Haskell could open his mouth, I says, "I calculate the pie to be worth less'n a dollar, but I'd be glad to buy it off you for that." I had saved up ten dollars and thirty-five cents which was hid in my bedroom.

"We are not in the pie-selling business," Rev. Haskell says, looking surprised again and maybe tempted.

"One pie don't make a baker," I says, "and one stolen pie don't make a thief."

Rev. Haskell scowled back at my old man and says, "What kind of creature you making out of this boy, Andy?"

"I don't know," my old man says. "He's doing it by himself."

Before I could say some more, Rev. Haskell says, "Now you just keep quiet and let Fred talk."

"Go on, get it over with," Fred says.

"That's not what I want to hear, Frederick," Rev. Haskell says, "as you very well know. You *know* what I want to hear."

But I guess he didn't because Fred went all pale and panicky and give me a quick look and even glanced out the door like he might make a run for it.

"I am not concerned about the pie," Rev. Haskell says, mostly to me. "I am concerned about the Foul Spirit behind this act, and the Foul Spirit has only one name."

"That's right," Fred says, lighting up and smiling and acting relieved. "I done the Devil's work."

"The foul spirit behind it was we was both hungry," I says.

Rev. Haskell crossed his arms and tapped his foot and glared at me. "Are you contradicting your pastor, Junior?"

"Have you decided what punishment Fred's going to get?" I says.

That jarred him off his course a little, and he says, "That's a family matter. What's it got to do with you?"

"Because whatever it is, you'd ought to cut it down by a third," I says. "If that was a family pie and you got three people in your family and it's even shares, you can't go switching Fred for stealing his own piece of pie. It ain't fair."

"What's right and what's wrong, what's fair and what's not, and what's the Devil's work and what's proper," Rev. Haskell says, starting to roll up loud, "isn't for you to judge. You'll take the word of your elders and betters."

My old man come into the room then and says, "You two go on out back and stay there till you're called for."

Me and Fred went out a little ways and squatted on our

hunkers to wait, not saying anything, and we could hear our fathers (which ain't in Heaven) talking a little in the kitchen, but pretty soon they wasn't talking no more, and when I crawled back and snuck a look, there they set, digging into the pie. Which was our lesson for the day.

Fred got switched good and proper (he told me later), but my old man just led me home, picking his teeth with his ivory toothpick, and didn't say nothing more about it, just looked at me peculiar for a couple days afterward till it wore off and he forgot.

3

———— • ————

But then the strange things begun to happen. My old man and Fred's come to some kind of agreement about us. We had both hit seventeen that same summer, having got through (kind of late) all the school there was in our town without being crippled or trampled to death, and as much extra as the teacher could scrape up, and they decided they was going to get us tutored instead of shipping us off to the nearest real high school (which there was only five of in the whole state).

What they done was get two men nobody'd ever seen or heard of before, a young lawyer named Bentley Mauger and a young preacher supposed to be right out of the seminary named Sam Pinkus, to trade off on us three days apiece, six days a week—Mauger for Law and Geography, Pinkus for

Religion and Latin, and anything else they happened to re-
member. And somehow or other out of the deal Fred was to
get to go to Harvard Divinity School, and since old Rev.
Haskell didn't have no more money than a dirt farmer, I
guess he must of had something on my old man. Either that,
or my old man figured it was worth it getting a boy from a
religious family to dog me back East when the great time
come.

I could tell right off these two tutors was in the wrong
trade: Sam Pinkus was a short, squatty, puffed-out, smily
kind of hand-grabber always making you think everything's
just fine and you're hot on the right track, even though you
maybe just come up with a hollow "I dunno" to the conjuga-
tion of some Latin noun or other—I can't think of none right
now, but, yes, like *aqua* which means "water"—but he'd be
nodding and pursing up his lips like you come close to hit-
ting it and only needed a little jogging and you'd be true as a
trivet. That kind of man is got no future in the preaching
business if you ask me. You start making people think
they're right all the time—even half the time—and where
are you? You're out of a job, which was exactly why Pinkus
was setting and sweating under the meeting-house roof (it
was made out of old tin cans hammered flat and laid on like
shingles) three afternoons a week with the two of us squirm-
ing and mumbling on the bench in front of him.

People in Wyoming wasn't too high on preachers any-
ways, but if they was going to have one, they didn't want no
roly-poly youth with peach fuzz on his first chin and sweat
on his second, who acted like he'd glad-hand the Devil him-
self if he'd only help teach Sunday School.

But Bentley Mauger, who was supposed to be reading law
over at Lawyer Shanklin's cubbyhole up above the Land
Office, looked even more like a preacher than Fred's old
man. He didn't have no gray hair yet, but he had one of

them dark, solemn, deep-looking faces, just as thick at the jaw as it was up at his bulgy cheekbones. He looked like he knew you a durn sight better'n he wanted to, and he was always working at some kind of knob in his throat, like he had it half swallered but didn't know if he could trust it in his stomach. He might of made a good prosecutor, but they didn't give no sugary-sure county jobs like that to young-sters. Mauger was over six foot and slim and kind of bent forward as if he couldn't believe what his big hairy ears had commenced to tell him you was saying. If he'd been fonder of talking, there wouldn't of been no congregation in Wyo-ming he couldn't of scared Hell out of.

So there they set, plugging away at their futures, trying to get in good with my old man and Fred's old man, jamming theirselves deeper and deeper into the wrong-shaped hole. It was about the only thing I learnt that whole first part of the summer, except how to spit between my front teeth.

4

———— ● ————

Most people think young men in the West get to be cowboys automatic, they just breathe it in along with the dust. But Fred and me was like city boys, though we didn't live in no city. There was lots of horses and wagons in the street in good weather and cattle looking for shrubbery to eat in bad weather and hogs doing nothing in all kinds of weather, and we had saloons and a mess of ornery people drifting in and out of that side of town and even some gunfights, which I had never actually seen happen though I did see some of the results going by in Clifford Tolt & Sons Undertakers buckboard.

But none of that meant I could ride a horse. I didn't *have* no horse. My old man owned two—one for saddle and one for our surrey—but I never got close to neither of them except with a currycomb. I didn't own no gun neither, not even a busted one for a toy, and I had never shot one off, and the same goes double for Fred. There was a law you couldn't carry one no more in Wyoming, but half the people did anyways, even my old man kept a small nickel-plated Derringer inside his coat "in case of emergencies," he said, by which he meant if somebody who'd got beat in court went out and liquored himself up and come hunting.

So if I couldn't ride or shoot and didn't have no sombrero (I had a corduroy cap and a flat-topped Canton straw hat and a big black wool cap like a candle snuffer for winter), I couldn't rightly claim to be no cowboy. But I thought about it oncet in a while—all of us did, even Fred—but my old man wouldn't even hear the start of an idea like that.

One of the times I thought about it most was that same summer, and I was out riding on my Gent's Utah bicycle. I'd held out for a good one because I'd seen some of them cheap ones with their frames broke to pieces in no time. And it turned out I was right, too, because no sooner did I get it out of the crate and put together than my old man wanted to get on it himself out behind the stable where nobody could see. He lost interest in about a minute and didn't bother me no more after he got his pants leg unhooked from between the chain and the sprocket, but if I hadn't had a good one, I wouldn't of had none at all when a man the size of Pa got through.

Well, I was out at the edge of town the next day, which wasn't very far—you could stand in the middle of town and look east and west on Main and north and south on First and see four kinds of prairie all looking the same. The streets had been baked good and hard, and all the ruts was wore down almost flat, and there wasn't much wind to speak of, and a high haze was keeping the sun from making the handlebars too hot to hang on to, and I felt pretty good. Our tutoring had petered out for another day, and Fred was standing way back yonder by our house, trying to watch me and hoping for a ride (preachers' sons couldn't afford no $40 bicycle, and my old man said he couldn't neither), and I was out at the west edge of town past the railroad tracks with nothing much between me and the Continental Divide but bronco grass. I'd never been no further from town than this, there being no reason for me to go.

The street turned into a wagon trail there, with ruts still deep and crooked from the spring, and I felt like taking it. I even rode a little ways on it, trying to steer clear of trouble, but my front wheel got caught in one of them deep slashes a wagonwheel can make, and it tipped me over. I hoped I was too far away for Fred to see good, and while I was cleaning myself off and hoping the housekeeper wouldn't see the scuffs on my elbows, along come a cowboy on a horse.

Least, I thought it was a cowboy when I first seen him coming, but when he come close and I got the sun out of my eyes, I could see he wasn't much older than me. He had on bearskin chaps that looked hotter than blazes and two kind of bandannas, red and blue, and he was dusty-faced.

He stopped off to the side about ten feet and says, "What's that thing?"

"That's a Gent's Utah bicycle," I says. "The best there is."

"What's it good for?" he says.

I didn't like the tone of voice, but I didn't have much idea what to do about it, so I just kept on checking my wheels.

"Is that there a stallion, a mare, or gelding?" he says and give a kind of clickety laugh.

"Least I don't have to clean up no horse apples after it," I says. "And I don't have to hustle no hay for it neither."

"How's she do uphill?" he says.

Since there wasn't no hills to speak of as far as you could see, I didn't have to worry none about that. "It not only goes up, son," I says, "but coming down you can take yourself a nap, and it'll run all by itself."

"Who you calling *son?*" he says, frowning and giving his raggedy-looking little pinto a twitch on the reins. "You ain't old enough to blow your own nose yet."

"I'm seventeen," I says, wishing I'd made it eighteen.

He give that laugh again. "Ain't you playing pretty far away from home, *son?*" he says. "Little bit more and your ma won't be able to hear you. Then if you was to get cornered by a prairie dog, why, you'd be a goner."

He kept looking left and right while he talked, and I knew his kind of a josher: when they don't have their dumb sidekicks with them to whoop it up, they forget what to say next. I says, "That's a pretty mean-looking jack rabbit you're riding there yourself. Did you catch her or did she catch you?"

The kid starts to frown again, and he tilts back his pointy-crowned sombrero, showing the clean strip high on his forehead between the dust and his hair. "I just want to get something clear, sonny," he says. "Are you looking for a fight?"

He had a carbine in a saddle holster, but no hand gun—at least not so's I could notice—and I didn't feel like being afraid of him. I'd sort of got out of the habit over the last year because being afraid took up too much time. "I got no cause to fight," I says.

"Then how's come you're giving *me* cause?" he says. "You're going to get your nose rolled up."

"All I done was—"

"I don't care what you think you done," he says. "You get on home now." He made a little shooing flick with one hand, and his pinto put her ears back and shied. "This here's open range, and it's for men only."

"I got as much right here as anybody," I says, checking my handlebars to make sure they was straight. "I ain't no steer and I ain't no cayuse, and you can't tell me where to go and you sure as blazes can't make me go there neither." I didn't look at him or raise my voice. Arguing makes me shy because I don't like to bother people.

He got a short rein on that fidgety little paint and got her to come at me nose first, ready to swing a flank around, like he was going to cut me out of a herd. But I could tell the horse didn't like the looks of my Gent's Utah bicycle none, so when they got too close to me, I give a triple flip to the bell on the handlebars, and that pony went about fifteen feet sideways in one swoop, her head raring up till her ears was almost in the kid's lap. He got her stopped there, and he looked all waked up and perked up and mad now, not tired no more.

"You're going to pay for that," he says.

"How much do you figure on charging me?" I says. "If it's more'n two cents a foot, I can't afford it."

I shouldn't of said that because now there wasn't nothing left for him to do but get down off that pony and fight. But I never could pass up a wise remark. Even when he was licking me for it, my old man would admit a good lawyer was never at a loss for an answer. And he also said losing your temper was the most sinful luxury you could think up, but *seeming* to lose it was one of the finest tools of the trade.

Anyway, I could see this here kid had lost his temper altogether. He couldn't even get off his horse right, and he had to hop along with it a couple of yards with one boot stuck in the stirrup. And the pinto was getting sick and tired of all this commotion: she'd just been jogging along for miles probably, not having to think about nothing, and now all of a sudden there was this machine and this jouncing around and all this chiyukking. He couldn't hold her still when he got all the way off. He kept wanting to turn and look at me and get his eyes hard-looking, but he had to tussle with the reins mostly instead.

And then because there wasn't no tree or bush in sight, just some little old spindly greasewood not much more'n ankle high, he had to bend way over and tether her to one of them and test it to make sure the roots wasn't rotten. So by the time he could give me his undivided attention, he was good and riled, yet kind of ashamed of himself too.

And now he had another problem because he seen he wasn't quite as big as me, least not as tall, not even with them hobbledy two-inch heels under him, and I could see he was wishing he hadn't bothered.

He come five feet away and stopped and spraddled bow-legged and says, "Go on now. Ain't nobody going to see you run, boy. Except me."

"That's one too many," I says. But I didn't know where to put my bicycle. There wasn't nothing to lean it against, and I hated to lay it down and get grit all over the chain or have it be tromped on, so I just hung onto it.

He says, "You going to take off some of them Sunday clothes and put up your dukes?"

I had on my four-button plaid bicycle suit, brand new, and I wasn't about to take it off for man nor beast. I wheeled the bike a little ways off the road and let it sink over on some low bushes, then come back and put 'em up the way I seen Gentleman Jim Corbett do it on a poster (though he'd just got beat down in Nevada by somebody named Fitzsimmons), and the kid looked at me kind of surprised.

I pulled my cap down tight and says, "Come on, cowboy," which was a big surprise to *me*. I didn't have nothing to fight about.

He come a couple of steps closer, brushing the dust out from under his eyes and squinting at me, and I knew for dead certain he wasn't no more'n eighteen. A long sharp face dished-in at the sides and a pointy chin.

"Who's your next of kin?" he says.

"None of your beeswax."

He shook his head, smiling kind of nervous. "Can't you see that carbine on my saddle, boy? Don't you know better'n to mess with an armed man? What's to keep me from saving energy and just plunking you one?"

"You make a move for it now," I says, "and I'll scare off that little skewbald rabbit of yours and you won't catch her till next week." Least, that's what my voice said. It come out of my mouth, and I figured right then I better not go down around the pool hall or the Checker Casino no more till I found out who was doing all this big talking inside me.

I could tell he was thinking about it: he was looking back at that bitty piece of greasewood he'd tied her to and thinking how tired he was. "Well, I'd have me a nice new bicycle to chase her with," he says.

But that was just talk. So I says, "I got no quarrel with you unless you start to mess with me." My old man always said to leave a man a way out of a corner if you wasn't in the market for corners. "I didn't say nothing about you."

He turned right around and went for his horse, and I opened my mouth to holler and spook it, but I stopped. He durn near did the job himself: the little paint had that bush out of the ground by the time he caught hold of the reins, and he just barely held it. But he didn't pull out the carbine. He just swang up into the saddle and gentled her down halfway, looking tired. He says, "I guess I just ain't used to the sight of the likes of you. Been out on the range too long, and I forget what people's like in town. And I'm too tuckered out to fight. But I'll be around for a week, so any time you want some, just ask for Lassiter over at Flank's boardinghouse."

I got my bike back on the road, and the pony shied from it again.

"You better go first," the kid says. "I don't want this thing to think you're coming up her tail."

"I'm Jackson Holcomb," I says.

"Oh for godsake," he says. "You Andy Jackson Holcomb's boy? You trying to get me hung?"

"My old man don't hang nobody," I says. "There's no money in it."

The kid laughed a short real laugh then and leaned one elbow back on his slicker-covered bedroll.

I got on my bike and started back toward town, trying not to wobble too much because I knew he was looking. I could see Fred way in the distance, peering at me with one hand shading his eyebrows, and I wished it was his bicycle. I didn't ride it even oncet after that.

5

——— • ———

Sam Pinkus and Bentley Mauger, our fearless tutors, was supposed to be getting us sprouted into preaching and law-yering, but the main trouble was, Fred was doing better at law books than me and I was doing better at the Bible than him. And neither of us wanted to talk much, which is what you've got to do *mostly* if you're going to get into either one of them fields. My old man and Fred's too was always call-ing them "fields" or "fields of endeavor" or "walks of life," and whenever they'd do that, I'd see myself walking in a field some place, just walking in the grass, not preaching, not arguing, not bailing nobody out, not praying over the sick nor bribing no juries.

The truth is, me and Fred—especially me—didn't know what we wanted to be. It was too soon. I couldn't see why they was all in such a rush to get us to Harvard and start suffering.

One of the Psalms I learnt by heart—I could learn twicet as many twicet as fast as Fred if I felt like it, but I didn't really feel like it—said in it: "My heart is smitten, and withered like grass; so that I forget to eat my bread. By reason of the voice of my groaning my bones cleave to my skin. I am like a pelican of the wilderness: I am like an owl of the desert. I watch, and am as a sparrow alone upon the house top." And the rest was all about having a bunch of enemies, and it wasn't bad, but I liked the part about the birds best. I was getting like that myself, going off my feed and groaning whenever I had to do any chores and feeling like I was all alone and different, yet at the same time it seemed like there was too many people around. And it might seem funny, but I had the notion some of them might be my enemies too, which ain't supposed to be Christian.

Fred was just so glad to get aholt of anything that wasn't the Bible, he ate his way through them lawbooks like a rat going through a sack. The way our tutors taught us was mostly to tell us to read something, then go away and sleep (Pinkus used to get the cushion from Fred's old man's preaching chair, the only cushion in the place, and prop it up in a corner for his head; Mauger didn't need no encouragement like a cushion: he could fall asleep with his eyes open, anywhere, any time) and then come back (or with Mauger, come *to*) and ask us what we'd read. If one of us had happened to do any studying, that one'd start telling about it or explaining it a little, and Pinkus would nod and smile and chuckle and look real pleased and Mauger would frown and squint and sneer, but no matter what we said, whether we was in the meeting house with Pinkus or up in my old man's bake oven of an office with Mauger, they'd quit listening pretty soon and let it go at that.

Now, anybody who's ever been to school can tell you, you can't treat young men like that and expect them to work. At first we took turns, like I said, and then before a week was up we found out we didn't have to know *nothing* about the subject we was supposed to of studied up on. So from then on, that's just about exactly what we knew.

Fred started it, though he didn't do it apurpose. Pinkus had him stood up for Latin and asked him to decline the word for something or other—I don't remember what it was, and I didn't know then, neither—and while he was waiting, Pinkus strolled away to the window with his back to us, which even a *half*-witted teacher can tell you is a big mistake, and Fred, who hated Latin even worse than me, catches my eye and mouths *What?*, and I shrugs and mouths back *Damn if I know,* and Fred says out loud, "Damfino, damfinere, damfinitus, damfinitum," or something like that, and Pinkus nods and smiles and yawns and goes on to the next thing.

So when I seen that happen, I quit cold. No more book learning except when I felt like it, which wasn't too often during the short time that was left, and after a while Fred come to believe it too, and he eased off, though I could tell sometimes he was really studying when he pretended he wasn't.

We fed them two tutors every kind of wrong answer we could think up, as long as it didn't sound too raw, and they swallered them just as easy as pickled beets. They didn't know nothing about geography (outside of Wyoming, Montana, and Kansas) or history or Latin or law (except how much jail you can get for doing this or that kind of a crime) or English or anything else we was supposed to be soaking up.

I started using this here very confident voice and made up a Revolutionary War fight called the Battle of Muddy Bottom, fit by General Pittsburgh and General Shadrack on a river bottom in Pennsylvania, and Mauger didn't even blink. And I made up a brand-new book of the Bible called the Book of Isaac and throwed in my own ideas about what Isaac done to Abraham to get back at him for almost slitting his throat like a sheep, and Pinkus took it all in without a ghost of a fuss. At first Fred shied off, saying it was blasphemery (that was one of his old man's favorite words, and he used to hit it hard and hang on to it whenever it come up in a sermon), but pretty soon he was making up extra verses in the middle of things or reciting them half backwards or sticking in sayings like "Thou shalt not covet thy father and thy mother," and Pinkus didn't seem to mind that neither.

But the fun of it had wore off in a few days, and all we had left to keep our minds busy was wondering who Pinkus and Mauger really was, because it was a sure certain cinch they wasn't no divinity student and no lawyer. Fred knew more about churching (without wanting to) than Pinkus, and I knew ten times more about the law (without wanting to) than Mauger. What we couldn't figure out was how they come to fool Fred's old man and mine so easy, when they couldn't fool us worth a blame.

So me and Fred decided we'd try and draw them out, casual like, and see if there was *anything* they knew more about than us, commencing with Pinkus because he didn't have no temper to speak of. Well, we fished around and fished around, first off trying Pinkus on the law in case I'd been right and they'd got theirselves switched into the wrong pews, but Pinkus didn't know a tort from his Uncle Mort, and when we switched Jesus into the Book of Job for Mauger, he didn't move a muscle, so that wasn't it.

Then one day Fred happened to mention how his old man wouldn't let him have no kind of gun at all because "Thou shalt not kill" and being a preacher's son and being individually responsible for bringing law and order to the West, and all the rest of that lecture every young man knows dang near by heart, though in my case being a judge's son didn't count much when it come time to muck out the stables. Well, Pinkus started slow and agreeable, but then he got going on the kind of rifles you could trust and how come the new .30 caliber Winchester repeater was a better all-purpose weapon than the Marlin, and how you should always have a "take down" rifle so's you can keep it good and clean and safe. And pretty soon he was off on revolvers, being a great believer in the Colt double-action, self-cocking .45 caliber revolver because if you're going to hit something you don't want to give it a little-bitty tap on the shoulder, like some of them short-barreled small-caliber guns.

He caught himself after a couple minutes and made a big fuss about agreeing with Fred's old man, and we went back to hashing up the Bible again. But we knew we was on to something now. And when I tried it on Mauger (most of the time Fred was scared to open his mouth around that lanky, scratchy-bearded, scowling man) I put it to him like a law case where somebody'd drawed on an unarmed man and made him do something illegal, and Mauger woke up for a minute and said anybody dang fool enough to go unarmed when everybody else was packing iron didn't count for nothing anyways, especially when there was pocket guns like the Colt .32 which you could keep on you like a piece of loose change. But he dried up in a hurry, and we was back to reading lawbooks, which in my case meant daydreaming mostly.

And the very next day I hit on horses with Pinkus, sort of by accident. I was thinking about that young cowboy I'd brushed with out on the edge of town, and I asked Pinkus right in the middle of a Psalm what makes some horses wild and shy and some others slow and steady, and what could you do to take the jitters out of a horse. And you'd of thought he'd just hired the hall and was going to deliver Lecture Number One to the Horse Dealers' Association. I didn't understand half of what he was talking about because in them days I only recognized the parts of a horse if somebody had one there to point at.

His talk was all full of hock and wither and barrel and girth and loin and so many hands for this and so many hands for that, and then something about curb and spavin and all like that. And old chubby Pinkus had a faraway look in his squinty eyes, like he was seeing just the one he wanted, and as a finisher he hit Preacher Haskell's lectern a good boom with his fist and denounced white horses with pink skins and pink eyes just like they was backsliders or Papists. Then he seemed to catch himself, and we squared around to some no-account geography where Fred made up a new country between France and Spain till he couldn't think of no more names for things, and I had to add a couple. But Pinkus was off at the window, thinking about horses and just nodding at whatsoever we said.

So we tried sneaking horses into our lessons with Mauger, and he jerked out of his trance long enough to say, "Never trust no horse with an arched nose, a bulgy forehead, small flat eyes, and a rump like a goose," which was a fair description of Mauger, except he was pretty lean for a goose.

6

———— • ————

That evening me and Fred met in our stable after supper for
our regular "study" session, which it wasn't but a joke for
loafing around a little without getting bothered about red-
ding up dishes or messing with some other chore (Fred
didn't have no handy sisters neither), and we begun to guess
what we was up against: a young lawyer who didn't know
nothing about the law, and a young preacher who didn't
know his Bible from *Moore's Almanac*, both of them even
more ignorant of schooling than me and Fred, and both of
them hot and high on guns and horses. Well, it didn't take us
long to romance it: they was desperadoes hiding out till the
posse scattered and the reward posters got bleached off the
telegraph poles.

But then Fred had even a better idea, which don't happen

any too often. He was straddling the wagon tongue, and staring down at the messy straw like there was something in it he had to memorize, and rubbing his blue-denim shirt kind of thoughtful, and he said, "Them two's in cahoots. Fixing to rob this town. In disguise till they get it all planned and the rest of the gang shows up."

I had to admit I liked that fine.

Fred says, "Should I tell my old man?"

That was like Fred: if he ever did have a good idea, he was sure to have a bad one right after it. "What's going to happen then?" I says. "If they find out our tutors don't know nothing, maybe they'll get us a couple that do. *Then* where are we?"

We set thinking about it awhile. Then Fred says, "But we can't let them go ahead and rob something."

"Why not?" I says.

"It's against the law and the Ten Commandments," Fred says.

Which just goes to show you about Fred. I tried to think fast. I says, "How'd you like to be numbered among the False Accusers? How'd you like to have a suit for slander slapped on you and take every cent you got?"

"I ain't got any to take," Fred says.

But I could see I had him worried. "Don't you know you need evidence, you ignoramus?" I says. "It has to stand up in a Court of Law. The innocent is innocent until proved guilty."

"That ain't what you said about your old man's court," Fred says.

"Never mind what I said. Let's stick to the facts, which when you look at it we got dang few of."

Fred says, "What's going to happen come September and my old man asks me to start reciting what I learnt?"

I went to the stable door and looked out both ways along

the hard-packed dirt lane beside our house to make sure no-body was listening. The sun was deep red on the other side of town. I says, "Don't borrow trouble," which is a favorite saying of my old man's housekeeper, and it means *Shut up and keep out of the way.*

"He'll skin me," Fred says.

"Not if we save the town from getting robbed," I says.

Fred looked doubtful about his own idea. "You think they're really crooks?"

"Well, they sure ain't tutors."

"What could they be fixing to rob?"

"The bank, the railroad office, the Checker Casino—how should I know? What would *you* rob if you had your pick of the town?" I says.

"Stealing's a sin."

"Well, can't you just pretend?"

Fred thought awhile and scuffled his foot like he didn't want to think what he was thinking, then he says, "The rail-road office."

"Why?"

" 'Cause I'd have fewer people riled with me when I was done," he says.

"Everybody ain't as big a scairy-cat as you," I says. "Look at all the banks that get robbed. *Some*body does it."

Fred says, "I got to get to the prayer meeting and pump the organ. Mrs. Watts has got arthuritis in her foot." And he slipped out the stable door and started home, looking like he didn't want to mess with robbers, and I could see it was up to me to find out what was going on.

So I went back in the house, slipping through the kitchen and past the pantry, while the housekeeper was rattling the lids back onto crocks, and through the dining room, and I could tell by the green light coming out of the study door my old man was in there. He'd come home late that afternoon, and I'd got to eat in the kitchen before him, which was what I like to do instead of having to sit up straight and speak when I'm spoken to and keep my napkin off the floor and hold my elbows in and shut my mouth when I chew and keep both feet flat on the carpet where God meant them to be. He'd only nodded at me from the doorway.

I knew I was taking a chance bringing up a touchy subject like the tutoring, not knowing no more about the Law than I ever had, but I figured I could always be taken sick and get out of it, especially when he was rooted down with a brandy snifter and a long stogie.

I hung around the door a few seconds till he took notice of me, then I says, "Pa, can I talk to you?"

"You may," he says, taking a long draw on the stogie and letting the smoke come out slow, the way it does out of a chimbley when there's no wind. "And kindly come through the door while you're at it. Doors was meant to be passed *through*. If you stand in a door, you are rendering it useless except as a picture frame for yourself, and you ain't old enough to be a worthy subject for a tableau. Nor the right sex neither."

He talks like that, and why it don't drive them people in court crazy, I don't know. Maybe it does after a while. I says, "I been thinking about my future."

"I told you, in so many words, to sit down, Junior," he says. "Now are you going to do it?" He creaked forward in the platform rocker and gave me a big long look, raising and sinking his bushy silver eyebrows.

So I went and set on the little wooden step stool he used to use to reach the top bookshelf till he slipped off and sprained both ankles. It was the nearest thing to the door. "I was wondering exactly what kind of a lawyer you was figuring on me being," I says. "There's lots of different kinds."

"I am aware there's different kinds," he says. "You'll have

plenty of time to decide when you're at Harvard." He dunked the butt end of the cigar in the brandy and then give it a swirl between his big lips. "Your perfessers can help you on that score, I hope."

"What kind would you say Mr. Mauger is, for instance," I says, getting the words out before I could tangle them up thinking about them.

"Well," says my old man, looking like a judge with his dark cravat and his pearl stickpin and his black suit and his pale-blue striped fancy duck vest, "according to his credentials, I'd say Mr. Mauger is a common or garden-variety country lawyer fresh out of the pod. Why?"

"I just wondered."

"Has he been learning you anything yet?"

"I reckon so," I says. "You'll have to ask *him*," which I thought was a pretty shrewd way to get myself praised because any tutor in his right mind would brag about a pupil if he wanted to get paid.

But I should of known I couldn't sidetrack my old man that easy. He says, "I was asking *you*. What you been learning?"

"Torts," I says. "And procedure." I could think of them right off, but needed to change the subject quick. "Is Mr. Mauger from around here some place?"

"No, he's from Illinois."

Because during one of my "history" recitations I'd had George Washington marching through Illinois toward Georgia and Mauger hadn't batted one of his dark little eyes, I now had leave to doubt he was from there, but I didn't say so out loud. In fact, my old man had said *Illinois* kind of fast and a little too loud, like he was being contradicted, which he don't care for, so I knew I had to change the subject. But I couldn't resist one more try, so I says, "Do you think Mauger's going to be a good lawyer?"

My old man took a deep breath out of the brandy glass, letting his nose hang over the edge, then took a little sip on top of that. "Why does Mr. Mauger's future matter to you?" he says, looking dead still like a bull watching somebody sit on a fence.

"He's my tutor, ain't he?" I says, acting hurt.

Calming down a little, my old man says, "One of these days he's going to learn you not to say *ain't*."

"He says *ain't* himself." And so does my old man, but I'll never hear nobody tell him so.

After setting his chair to rocking, my old man says, "Anybody studies hard and learns people can be a good lawyer."

Which was a joke because I hadn't seen Mauger crack a book once, unless he was doing it on the sly.

"And after that," my old man says, "all you need is luck, a clean start, and maybe a good connection or two. You just implant that in your memory, Junior, and you won't go wrong."

"Are you a good connection, Pa?" I says.

"Son," he says, smiling slow and deep and kind of secret like he'd just inhaled the stogie and the brandy both at once, "I am like a railroad junction. If anything or anybody wants to pass through here on the way to profit or preferment, he or it has got to go through me. I am the light and I am the way, and when that there light turns red, everything comes to a screeching halt or there's going to be an accident." He let out a deep chuckle like a cough. "I am the red light and the right of way both. And you could do a whole lot worse than be a railroad lawyer, I can tell you that."

"Pa, I ain't so sure I want to be a lawyer at all." It was out before I could haul it back, and I got ready to get off that stool and out the door in a hurry.

He had a thick frown on his face as he leaned forward. "You're going to Harvard, and you might as well make up that little half-baked pie you got inside your head right now. Harvard."

"Oh, I'll go all right," I says, "but I mean maybe I wasn't cut out to be a lawyer."

"You wasn't cut out to be nothing. You was born like a man, and a man is not a suit of clothes, Junior. He is what's *inside* them clothes." His voice was deep and big now, filling up the whole room. "A man can grow into his own dream, no matter how broad it is in the shoulders, no matter how baggy it is in the seat. If a man can't do it no other way, a man can *eat* himself into the right size, by God. Now what kind of fool notion you picked up?"

I couldn't tell him I was thinking about being a cowboy, not when I didn't even know how to ride. And cowboys was one of the lowest forms of life in our town, even on payday. "I was just trying to speak my mind," I says.

"What mind?" he says, then calmed down a little. "You been sniffing around the girls?"

I knew I was blushing. "No."

"You only got to study a few years, and the first thing you know, it's all over, and you can do what you damn well please. Don't let girls get in your way now, they'd mess you up for sure."

He was talking low and sincere, like he knew what he was talking about without having to holler. He was staring at me hard, and I kept still, not letting him catch my eye.

He says, "I've been meaning to give it to you," and he reached past the decanter on the table next to him, picked up a little package, and unwrapped a small beet-red book, pausing to thumb it a minute like he wasn't quite sure about it.

Least it wasn't no lawbook, not at that size, so I didn't mind getting up and taking it when he held it out. The title was stamped on the cover: WHAT A YOUNG BOY OUGHT TO

KNOW: *Self and Sex Series,* "Purity and Truth," by Sylvanus Stall, D.D.

"You don't have to read it all right away," my old man says, kind of nervous. "Just if you should happen to need some advice. There was another one called WHAT A YOUNG MAN OUGHT TO KNOW, but I didn't want to rush you none."

It was the first time I ever heard him hint he might be running short of advice on his own hook, but I seen what he meant, and I got out of there before he could start talking about my ma.

7

———— • ————

So the next day while Pinkus was napping in the corner of the meeting house with his head jammed into the preacher's seat cushion and me and Fred was pretending to read the Book of Proverbs, I whispered to Fred and told him we had to follow Pinkus after the lesson and find out where he lived and what he was doing.

Fred turned white and shook his head and glanced over at Pinkus's bulgy cheeks and his short fat legs sprawled out crooked on the floor. "No," he says.

Now I had chose Pinkus deliberate instead of Mauger to start with because he was less scary, but I guess he didn't seem less scary enough to Fred. I didn't say no more about it, but when Pinkus come jerking and sputtering out of his nap and had got his long, straw-colored hair combed back in place with his fingers and had give us a little quiz on the Book of Numbers—he'd forgot which book he'd told us to mull over, but it didn't make no difference because he couldn't tell one from the other anyway—I was set firm to trail him, whether Fred come along or not.

Pinkus bustled off like he always did, setting his flat-top straw hat square on his head, looking cheery and business-like in the same tight, smudged brown suit he'd been wearing ever since we first laid eyes on him, trotting along on his high-heeled, pointy-toed, ankle-high, laced-up brown shoes toward the middle of town.

And I took off after him, on the same side of Main Street at first but not crossing over when he did, and pretty soon, when we was both on the boardwalks in front of the three-block string of stores, I could keep in the shade along the front of the barbershop and the millinery store and Plunkett's Dry Goods, while Pinkus was stepping fancy past the hardware and the Sunflower Café. Fred was bobbing along behind me, sometimes lagging way back and sometimes nearly catching up and whispering questions and warnings and all kind of stuff, but I didn't pay him no mind. If I learnt anything yet, it's if you want to have an adventure, you got to concentrate on it, because if you start letting your attention wander and start listening to a lot of fool questions, you're going to snap awake all of a sudden and find you lost it, and there ain't no adventure.

So when Pinkus turned into the bank, I had my eye right on him, and when he come out still folding some greenbacks, I didn't miss a trick, and when he crossed the street, having to circle a hog stretched out in the last remains of a mud puddle, and went into the Checker Casino, I was on him.

And when he done that, I set down on the stoop in front of Brady's Cigar Store and thought about it.

While I was trying to think, Fred says in my ear, "Did you see that?"

"Yes," I says.

"What kind of a preacher'd go into a saloon?" he says, sort of awestruck.

"No kind," I says.

Fred went quiet then and set down beside me to wait, and I could tell he was probably running over in his mind some of the things his old man would say and do if he was to catch Pinkus near a whiskey glass and a card table.

After a minute, Fred says, "How we going to watch him now?"

A couple of wagons went by with dogs barking after them, while I turned it over and over. My old man's courthouse was just a block away, but if him or the Mayor or some attorney or somebody from the bank or some halfway respectable railroad man wanted a snort in the middle of the day—or any other time—all's they had to do was slip across the street to the Palace Hotel where the bar was dark and quiet and you could pretend you was having a business meeting. Pinkus wouldn't of attracted no notice in there, to speak of.

But going in the Checker Casino was an automatic sin, just as if a bell rang and a flag went up, unless you'd come in with an ax to smash it up or with a Bible to pray over the soiled doves that worked there. That's what Fred's old man called them, though they didn't look nothing like doves, clean or dirty, but like pretty girls with red and yellow and green dresses and face paint—which is another automatic sin—and I used to hang around the door just to hear them talk, till somebody told my old man. They don't talk dirty, just wild and silly. It don't amount to nothing.

Yet to hear the church ladies talk, you'd think them soiled doves was the wickedest creatures in Creation, luring young men (and even old-timers) to their Disgrace, Degradation, and Damnation. They keep the Disgrace mostly on the main floor, and the Degradation and Damnation up on the second and third floors, to hear the church ladies tell it, and I'd only got to listen when they was on the main floor—and near the front door at that—so maybe they talked different upstairs.

Anyway, Pinkus was in there, and he wasn't packing any Bible or hymnal or ax. I listened to the tinkly piano music floating catty-corner across the dusty street, and I didn't blame him for wanting to go in. All I have to hear is I can't do something or go some place, and right away I want to go there and do it.

"They got a back door," Fred says. "And maybe, if nobody's looking—" His eyes was wide and scared.

"What back door?" I says. "How's come you know about a back door?"

"I just happened to see it once," he says.

I'd used to hang around the *front* door and get caught, but maybe that's another difference with sons of preachers.

We found that door all right, but the trouble was it led out to the customers' privy and wash trough, and every time we'd get close and get our nerve up to go through and start spying, somebody'd come clomping out to use one or the other or both, and we'd have to duck back and pretend we was talking. But there got to be a kind of rhythm to it after a while, like they was timing each other so's not to interfere, and when one bushy-bearded bandy-legged old man went staggering back inside, I followed him close, not waiting to see if Fred was going to faint, cut and run, or come along.

None of the outdoor customers had been bartenders or soiled doves, so I figured we didn't have to worry right away, maybe they enjoyed inside privileges, which wasn't too much to expect considering the size of the regular monthly "fines" they was able to pay the city by way of the sheriff. And I went sailing along behind the old-timer, keeping my eye out for a place to hide. It was dim, dingy, and smoky-smelling in the hallway, and the dimmer the better, but when the old-timer started across a small back room full of card tables and chairs toward the big lit-up front room past some halfway-open sliding doors, I pulled up short and felt Fred bump into me. Then I ducked sideways and crouched behind a round card table tipped over on its side with one leg broke off. It wasn't too good a place, specially when Fred got scrunched in behind it too, but there wasn't no other choice. Ten feet away a flight of narrow steps went up to the second floor, and if anybody come down them, all they had to do was glance our way and we was done for.

But meanwhile we could peek around the edge of the table and get a fine view of Pinkus with one foot up on the brass rail and his straw hat tilted back, breaking four or five Baptist Commandments, which is slightly different from the ones Moses toted down the mountain. He had half a fat cigar in his little mouth and a double-shot glass in front of him which his hand couldn't reach but halfway around, and he had a soiled dove in a green-and-white dress leaning one of her elbows on his shoulder like he'd been set up there for her convenience. And whenever he took the stogie out of his mouth long enough, his lips spread out on both sides in a sweet grin like a cat coming up out of a lard pail.

Fred seen him too and commenced nudging me and gasping while he soaked up the view, probably hearing his old man's rip-snorting bell-ringing denunciation in the back of his head. Somebody lit into the piano which was out of sight behind the sliding doors, and Pinkus tapped his toe on the rail and had a shot at spitting some cigar juice into the blue japanned non-skid spittoon next to him, but it went down both his chins and onto his shoe, which just goes to show you how important it is to learn to spit proper when you're young. He got his face wiped off without dislodging his dove and pretty soon had his grin going again, good as new.

A man wearing baggy overhauls come through the back room past us and into the hallway, heading outside, and we had to duck and hope because there wasn't no way to get out of sight completely, though the windows was all shuttered and the light was bad. So for a while we had a dog's-eye view of the underside of a poker table which, aside from a couple of stray pieces of gum (one of them was Adam's Pepsin Tutti Frutti or my nose is a liar), had a king of spades stuck near one edge, and that is as good a way as any to get your table legs broke off.

Fred started whispering at me for us to get out of there while the getting was good, and I suppose it wouldn't of been a bad idea since we'd already got Pinkus pegged down and salted, but I had a feeling there was more to come and, besides, I kind of liked being in a genuine casino and hellhole, even if I wasn't exercising the rights and privileges of a paying customer. The law ain't my fault, and what goes on in casinos and hellholes ain't my fault neither, and it ain't my fault I was only seventeen, and What a Young Boy Ought To Know is what happens in places he's forbidden to see, because then he wouldn't be so dang nervous and het up about finding out.

By now things was getting on for sundown of a Thursday, and the noise was picking up a little, and it seemed sure they'd be lapping over into the cardroom before long. And there was also the little matter of getting home for supper or getting flayed alive, specially at Fred's house where if you didn't make it in time to say grace, you wasn't just *dis*graced, you was dis-suppered and dis-trousered and discommoded and dismissed. I didn't get many lickings any more myself, but I sure stood to miss out on most of the Bill of Rights.

Pinkus wasn't doing nothing new except to put away half

his whiskey and change to his other foot on the rail, and he looked good for another hour of grinning and winking and trying to keep his chest higher than the edge of the bar. The soiled dove wasn't having no trouble on that score: her chest just sort of fit natural over the edge of things.

"Let's go," Fred says in a low voice.

But another privy customer come into the back room just as the man in the baggy overhauls tromped out of the hallway, and they met halfway and had a little chat about bobwire, which was turning so popular about then I expected to see it strung all around the town any day now, and me and Fred had to duck and hold still. But as soon as they'd parted and clomped off, Fred was up and at 'em again.

"Let's go," he says. "I'm going."

In the last chapter of WHAT A YOUNG BOY OUGHT TO KNOW (it ain't a very long book, which don't exactly speak well for Sylvanus Stall, D.D., if that's the sum total of his ideas) it says, "The years of adolescence, which begin in boys at about the age of fourteen and continue until they are about twenty-five, are fraught with perplexities, trials, and much danger. It is during these years that most boys make mistakes and go wrong; some physically, some intellectually, some morally, and some in all three of these respects. These mistakes for the most part grow out of the ignorance of the individual." That's just a high-flown fly-blown way of saying, "Smarten yourself up as fast as you can." So I was bound and determined to do it, with or without Fred.

In the ceiling overhead, right about in the middle of the room where it couldn't serve no sane purpose as a ventilator, there was a wrought-iron grill about a foot and a half square, and I'd heard tell about such things. If I was to run a cardroom, I'd want a place where I could watch what was going on in it without having to parade around. And I knew, from peeking through the front door months ago, there was card tables in the big front room too, so why wouldn't they have another spy door in the ceiling up front? And right there was that little flight of stairs.

Without even pausing to breathe I slipped out from behind the table and was crouched halfway up the stairs before Fred says, "My Gawd, what're you doing?" sounding scairt.

I shushed him and kept going, and the stairs was snapping and creaking and would of sounded awful if the piano hadn't been jangling away, and I turned the doorhandle at the top and stuck my head through into a corridor laid out with flowery green carpeting all the way to the front of the casino and shut doors all along it like in a hotel. Nobody home. There was a lamp up ahead and a shaft of reddish sunlight coming through the front window, and then Fred was clutching at me from behind.

"We'll get shot," he says.

"What for?" I says. "Shhh!"

While he was thinking what for, I got the door closed and headed toward the front, trying to guess whereabouts the middle of the big barroom would be. I went fast on tiptoe, having had lots of practice sneaking around home when I'd wake up starving in the middle of the night, and I knew the quietest place was over next to the baseboards. I couldn't hear nothing behind the first three doors, but somebody was mumbling behind the fourth, so I hurried past and past a narrow staircase up, skipped another silent door, and stopped at the next which was only two doors from the front of the building. Fred was smack behind me, looking like he'd been shot in the chest five minutes ago: he was hanging onto his heart and his face was dead pale.

I knocked on the door nice and gentle and waited.

"You're loco," Fred says.

I got him up close—as soon as I was sure nobody was

coming to the door—and between him and the doorknob, one foot on each, I clumb up to the transom (which was painted green inside) and pushed it open all the way down flat. Nobody hollered, and I clumb up onto Fred's shoulders then, sprawling forward through the slot and got aholt of the inside lintel, trying to keep my weight off of the glass, but it was all awkward as the devil, and I finally had to just sort of flop over head-first and backwards, banging the carpeted floor pretty good on all fours but not breaking nothing but the silence. I knew that was going to make a pretty good boom downstairs, so I waited there, crouched till I heard them start talking and laughing again after a pause.

I heard Fred whispering away at me through the door like he was afraid I busted my neck, so I unlatched the door and tried to get him in before he roused up the whole second floor, that Hotbed of Degradation, which looked neat and tidy and slick enough to pass muster for a church social.

But when I tried to haul him inside, he wouldn't haul. I only got as far as one arm before I seen him looking down the corridor and grinning kind of sickly and giving that little dip of the neck that means *Howdy*.

A woman's voice says, "Well, well, well."

Fred don't look quite as old as I do, mainly because he ain't allowed to dress as old, and though he was wearing long pants, they never even come close to the tops of his shoes: it was like his old man (or whoever bought the clothes in that household where his ma never opened her mouth much) was trying to save Fred from the temptation of growing too big, so they always kept his clothes a kind of ideal size. And they was a hard lesson for Fred sometimes, specially under the arms and in the crutch. So I knew right away he'd look mighty strange to whoever was out there, even if he had a bundle of Laramie *Boomerangs* under one arm and was selling them from door to door.

I give him a good yank then, and finally he come stumbling through and I latched the door after, listening hard. The woman laughed sort of halfhearted, like she wasn't sure what she was laughing at, then pretty soon a door closed and I couldn't hear no more.

Fred was having a fit of the sweats and wanted to talk, but I shushed him and looked around. It was like a little office with a black-leather couch and a desk with pigeonholes and pictures of ordinary girls on the wall, not a one of them looking like a soiled dove, and a swivel chair and a black-leather easy chair with lion's claws and a side table with whiskey bottles. But in case we didn't have much time, I started looking for a flap in the carpet, and sure enough I found one right in front of the easy chair, and when I pulled it back, there was a trap door with a ring handle laid flat. I give it a steady haul, and it come up slow and easy and quiet.

And when I laid out on the carpet and put my elbows on the edge, I had a grand view of the whole length of the bar and maybe a third of the tables, and I seen right away the trap door was mostly for checking on how and whether the cash changed hands over the bar and what happened to it after that. I could only see one little card game off to the side, and the grill squeezed out most of the view when I looked that way.

Pinkus was still in his place, hanging onto the whiskey glass like it was a saddle horn, though from up above he was mostly straw hat, but he'd lost his soiled dove now, and in her place was a flat-topped, small-brimmed black hat with a little silver buckle, and I didn't have to look twice to know whose that was, since he hadn't taken it off indoors or out for two weeks, as far as I knew. Mauger had joined the party.

I leaned back and whispered to Fred, "What kind of a lawyer comes to the Checker Casino?"

He calmed down a little and held still. "No kind," he says.

"Then come and take a look at one," I says and made room for Fred to look.

After a minute of shaking his head in wonder, Fred leaned back and says, "Now what?"

"Now we wait."

"We found out what we come for," Fred says. "Let's get out before they catch us, and I got to get home to supper."

"We have to see who joins up with them, don't we?" I says. "Maybe it's a gang."

"Don't talk so loud, they'll hear you." By now Fred had squatted back on his hunkers, looking around the room and probably trying to imagine what Degradation was like. "Is this where they sin?"

"It don't look very sinful to me," I says.

"Me neither."

"Where's all the perfume and the veils and draperies?" I says, remembering sermons and whispers and tall tales at school and dreams. "Where's the fleshpots?" All's I could see was a slop bucket in the corner by the desk, and I knew sure as shooting that wasn't it. "Where's the silken curves and the luxurious Turkish cushions and the ripe taste of forbidden fruit?" I says, turning it on full blast but in a whisper.

Fred says, "Don't talk like that," looking worried and probably expecting to see the Handwriting on the Wall.

"Where's that air of utter abandon as he crushed his lips to hers?" I says, enjoying myself sort of, and not exactly quoting from the *Self and Sex Series*. There's more than one book in this world.

"Maybe we just got the wrong room," Fred says. "You should of seen what I seen in the hall." His eyes got big and dark. "She was wearing this thing with feathers all over it, and where there wasn't no feathers, you could see through to—you could see her."

"See what?"

"Well, I don't know," Fred says. "Her skin I guess."

"Much of it?" I was trying to get the picture in my head, but he wasn't giving me enough to go on.

"I seen most of her lungs," he says, looking desperate worried, like he knew already he wasn't never going to be able to forget.

I didn't even get to see them, and I knew *I* wouldn't. "Was she a good-looker?"

"I don't know," Fred says. "I want to go home."

I checked Mauger and Pinkus to make sure they wasn't doing nothing new, then lowered the trap and stood up. "What you need's a drink. Put some spunk in you." I'd had sips of brandy three different times when my old man left some in the bottom of the snifter, and once the washerwoman down behind the hotel give me a half a glass of beer for fetching her clothesprops, so I was familiar with spirits and wasn't scairt.

Fred stood up straight like it was time for hymn number 42 and looked plain shocked at me. "I belong to the Band of Hope," he says, as though that settled it final.

I went over to the table and pulled the stopper out of the nearest cut-glass decanter and sloshed a couple of fingers into a glass. It didn't smell like brandy, so I wasn't sure what it was, but I says, "Here's rye in your eye," and took down a half a gulp without losing track of it.

Fred stared at me like he expected Hellfire to jump up at my feet and start a barbecue.

"Mighty fine," I says, though to tell the truth it tasted worse'n Celery Malt Compound the Great Nerve Builder that the housekeeper made me take the first of every month. But I smacked my lips and breathed out now like it was a treat. "Come on, this'll give you courage. That's how come most people drink it."

"I took the pledge," Fred says, looking kind of sorry. "But I could sure use some courage."

"Well, then have a little snort," I says. "We can't stay here much longer."

Fred wiped his hands on his pants. "A little drink is just as much of a sin as a big one."

"Then you might's well have a big one while you're at it," I says, and poured him a good one in another glass. Then I opened the trap again and checked on Pinkus and Mauger who hadn't budged. Whispering, I says, "Which kind of them soiled doves you like best, Fred? Fat, thin, tall, short, medium, dark, light, redheaded?"

"I don't dwell on them," he says, coming over and taking a long look at the whiskey glass.

I finished off my drink, and for the first time I knew what people meant by saying something hit the spot, because that rye or whatever it was hit my spot (it's right below my rib cage in the middle) like a fist. I had to shut the trap door and cough a minute. And by the time I got everything straightened out and could see out of one eye, there was Fred standing by the liquor table with an empty glass on it, looking solemn.

But before I could ride him about it, we heard a commotion in the hall, and high voices was squawking and yammering at each other. Fred just stood there with his lips shut tight, not even hardly listening but looking like he was going to faint, and when the lock turned and the door banged open, there wasn't nothing to do. I didn't feel like jumping out a window.

A big fat woman was in the doorway with her hands on her hips and her elbows out and a slash of red paint on her mouth as wide as a bullfrog's and feathers as long as rooster tails sticking up out of the top of her sparkly blue dress. She hauled a skinnier, younger woman halfway into the doorway and says, "Now take a good look and don't be slandering your betters."

The younger woman, who must of been the one Fred seen because she sure didn't have much cover on her lungs, took a glance at us and says, "Well, how was I to know?"

"What you don't know can't hurt you," the fat woman says, "unless you go to opening your big mouth and letting out what you don't know, and then it can hurt you real bad." She had a loud hard voice that like to peeled the wallpaper. "You just mind yourself, Susie, or you'll have to invest in some store teeth."

The younger woman ducked away, and a couple others tried to stick their heads around the corner to see into the room, but the fat woman shooed them away. "Get back to work, little honeybees, you know where the clover's at. It ain't in here. Simon?"

A mean-looking pock-faced little guy wearing boots, jeans, and a tight black shirt squeezed past her into the room with us. He had on a sixgun and a beltful of cartridges and black hair stringing down his forehead. "Hold still, gents," he says.

He didn't have to tell me, and Fred didn't look like he was ever going to move again, staring off in the corner some place with his lips pressed tight. This little Simon clomped over and looked inside our jackets and touched our hip pockets, then shook his head at the fat woman, who was studying us over with her eyes squinted.

"Wait outside," she says, coming in through the door sideways and having to ease her chest past the jamb.

Looking disappointed, Simon clomped out on his high heels, and she slammed the door on him, but he was already bending over to the keyhole before she had it shut all the way.

She give us another long studying look. "Well, what's

your ambition, boys?" she says. "What do you want to be when you grow up?"

I didn't know what to say, and if he heard her, I guess Fred didn't neither. But I couldn't stand the silence, and the liquor had loosened up my mouth, so I says, "There's no cause to get mad. We didn't harm nothing, did we, Fred?" But he just stood still, looking hangdog.

The fat woman went to the desk, glanced over it, took a small brown cigarette out of a box, and lit up. "Taking a little look along the bar, I see," she says, nodding at the trap where the carpet was still pulled back. "See anything you fancy?"

"Just curious, ma'am," I says. "It's a common complaint. We wasn't planning on plucking no forbidden fruits."

"Doing what?" she says, looking blank.

"Your reputation led us astray, Miss Lulu," I says. "We just wanted to see what a garden of fleshly delights lay inside your doors." Because I knew who she was. I'd heard people catting and sniping and gossiping about her for a year or more, whenever it was I started listening about women. She was Lulu that the song was wrote about, and if she really done all them things the song said, she was a busy woman.

She set down slow in the swivel chair, which give a little screech, and blew some smoke through her broad flat nose. "Tell me more, boys," she says, "I'm just off the stagecoach, and I need a friend." She said it sour and squinted back and forth between us.

I never seen so much paint on one face before. There was even patches of blue under her eyebrows like a couple of shiners, and the rouge went all the way back to her ears, which was dang near an overnight trip. "So there's no call to stir up trouble," I says. "We'll be glad to get out peaceful."

"Oh, you will, will you?" she says. "Who's going to pay for

my whiskey—" she nodded at the table "—and who's going to fix my transom?"

It *was* hanging down sort of busted-looking. "I will," I says.

"Let's see the color of your money, sport," she says.

"I don't happen to have it with me."

Fred give a kind of grunt then like somebody had poked him in the belly, and he shook his head *no*.

"Well, I thought the sons of judges was better prepared than that," she says, ignoring Fred. "I thought they was responsible citizens ready to pay cash on the nail for their goods and services and their tomfooleries. You wasn't thinking about special privileges by any chance?" And she fixed her eye right on me, so's I couldn't squirm out from under.

"I can pay," I says. "I got a Gent's Utah bicycle I can sell any day of the week."

"Son," she says, "you are in a cathouse, up on the business floor, and you have broke into a private office and stole some whiskey. You and your friend here molested a working girl in the hallway, who pays her fines as regular as any sheriff could wish, and you happen to be in more trouble than you can ride out of on a bicycle."

"Excuse me," Fred says.

"I won't do no such a thing," she says. "You stay right where you are, till we figure out what we're going to do about this."

"We didn't molest nobody," I says.

"You did if I say so," she says. "If I say so, you hung from the chandelier in your drawers and sang 'After the Ball Is Over.' If I say so, you lost your cherry in a spittoon, or you bent over a crib and made ten dollars, or you ruint an underage bloodhound." She was talking louder and louder, and the room was shaking. "If I say the word."

"Excuse me," Fred says, starting for the door.

She didn't pay much attention to him, probably because getting out of a swivel chair was a full-time job, but Fred went right out the door, bumping Simon (who'd been stooped to get an earful) back against the opposite wall, then turning down the hallway and picking up speed.

Simon got his gun out of the holster without dropping it, but Lulu says, "Hold it. No shooting in my place. Just catch him." Then when Simon started running, she looked at me and says, "Don't you go running off now. I'd be willing to make a little noise at *your* price. Wasn't that Haskell's boy?"

"A stranger," I says. "We wasn't introduced."

She closed one of her hands around my wrist and maneuvered her factory-made cigarette with the other. "Well, Andrew Jackson Holcomb, Junior," she says, "does your daddy know you're out?"

I'd got near enough to the door before she caught my wrist to be able to hear the commotion down the hall, but now she wouldn't let me far enough to look. "He'll know all about it just as soon as I tell him," I says. "I like to keep the Judge well informed." The worst thing I could do would be to cost my old man money.

Up close, she smelled like a dead bouquet only stronger. "Oh, I see," she says. "And how much allowance does he give you for these here evening excursions?"

"I didn't say he knew, I said I was going to tell him," I says.

"Then you won't mind if I tell him too?" she says. "Your daddy gets mighty embarrassed by old friends sometimes. Maybe you just haven't seen how embarrassed he gets. I'll tell you something, sonny: when a man grows a big roll of fat across the back of his neck and has to chain his vest together in front and turns red easy, he's ripe for picking."

• 5 7 •

"How'd you know who I was?" I says.

"I know a lot of things I ain't supposed to," she says. "You'd be surprised."

By then I couldn't hear no noise in the hall to speak of, but Fred wasn't coming back neither. I should of been feeling scairt, but the slug of whiskey was working on me, I guess. It made me feel ten years older. Besides, Lulu didn't have no right to talk about other people's fat. She had a roll of it around her middle like a money belt and a sackful under her chin, and when she give me a little bump with one of her lungs, it felt like curds in cheesecloth. "My old man won't pay you nothing," I says.

"Never can tell when the dam's going to bust," she says. "And while we're at it, come on and have a little look around, Junior."

"I'd be much obliged if you'd just let me go home," I says.

"Might's well do a little of what you're going to get blamed for," she says. "Might's well be hung for a sheep as a lamb."

"I reckon the lamb'd rather be a sheep awhile before they catch him," I says.

"Come on now," she says, and hauled me out the door with her. Three soiled doves had their heads stuck out of doors along the hallway, looking toward the rear even though there wasn't nothing there to see. "Inside!" Lulu hollers, and they all ducked back before I could even see what they had on.

Just then, Simon come down the narrow staircase about halfway along the hall, looking tussled up and mean and worried, and he quick straightened his bandanna and spit red on the floor.

"You spit on my carpet once more," Lulu says, "and I'll make you lick it up. Where's that boy?"

After a pause while he was probably trying to think up

some other way to say it, Simon give up and says, "He got away."

"You're a right smart of help, you are," she says.

"You told me not to shoot," Simon says. "If I'd been let to wing him, he'd be right there on the floor."

"Bleeding on my good carpet," she says. "And what was you planning on winging him with?"

We all three stood there looking at his empty holster, and a soiled dove stuck her head out and took a look too. She had on a robe the color of cornmush, and it was coming apart all the way down to the bottom of the bowl. Lulu shooed her back in before I could memorize her perfect, and if only Psalms and old court cases and the capitals of the world could look like that, I'd have the whole Bible and whole shelves of law and the whole atlas in my head in a week.

"I dropped it," Simon says.

"That's too bad," Lulu says. "Was it too much trouble to squat down and pick it up again?"

He thought about that a few seconds, glancing at me. "I made a mistake, and the kid got aholt of it."

Lulu went dead calm then, not an inch of her body moving. Even her big colored feathers held still. "Where is he?" she says, very quiet.

"If I knew that, I wouldn't be standing here," Simon says, practically shouting. "I looked upstairs too, and I couldn't find him."

"Why'd you look upstairs?" she says. "Didn't he run *down?*"

"I guess he did, but he ain't down there now." Simon was sounding a lot quieter now.

"So now we got a boy with a loaded gun some place," she says. "Ain't that nice, Junior?"

I kept still, and Simon says, "Can I have a new one?"

Lulu had let her attention wander a little in order to concentrate on getting mad at Simon, and her grip wasn't as tight on my wrist any more, so when I give it a yank and stepped sideways, I was on the loose, and I didn't see any reason for sticking around. "Well, so long," I says. "Be seeing you."

Right away, Simon sprang into a crouch between me and the back door at the far end of the hall, and Lulu give a two-finger whistle louder'n a steam boiler, and I seen the head and shoulders of somebody coming up the back stairs to join the party. So I done the first reasonable thing that come into my head: I went up the narrow staircase to my left.

She made a slow lunge and grab at me and missed, sprawling head first on the steps and wedging herself between the railing and the wall and making a short loud unhappy noise like a sow being asked to budge over. She must of slowed down Simon, who probably didn't want to leave no footprints on her nice new dress, because when I got to the top, I was on my own, and I figured anything Fred could do, I could do better.

8

———— • ————

All my life I'd been waiting for something to think about—
something thick and swift instead of the ordinary dawdling
and creeping and grinding everyday—and here it was, com-
ing at me as fast as I could catch it. I was on the third floor,
guaranteed Damnation itself, and it didn't look no different
from the second, except maybe dimmer and smokier and
plusher. The walls had something dark red and kind of soft
on them like cloth, and the wall lamps had red glass in them,
mostly. There was the same passel of doors on both sides in
both directions, and one soiled dove was walking off toward
the back in a shift—at least, that's what it looked like, but
since it was pale green, it must of been something else. She
didn't turn her head.

I had to choose in a hurry, and as long as she was going

some place, I figured I might's well string along, and if it was a dead end, at least I'd have some company. I caught up with her in three lopes, and she give me a big look with her mouth open.

Simon wasn't up the steps yet, so I says, "Who ordered the champagne?" more to cover the noise of scrambling and cussing behind me than anything else.

"Who what?" the soiled dove says.

"Champagne," I says. If I couldn't look like a customer, I could look like an errand boy.

"I'll take it if it's going around," she says. "Where is it?"

Because I was empty-handed, I says, "I was supposed to pick it up."

We come to a turn in the hall, and when she went left, I did too—just in time, it sounded like, from the clomping in back of us. Looking puzzled, she says, "They don't keep it up here, they keep it in the bar."

"I mean I was supposed to pick up the empties," I says, wondering which door to dodge into.

"You better not let Lulu catch you messing around up here," the dove says. "She don't like her customers bothered, and neither do I. Go on, scoot."

She kept on going to a door at the end of the hall, and I pulled up short and tried two doorknobs while she wasn't looking, but they was both locked. And by now I could hear boots thumping on the carpet.

She hung in the doorway just long enough to say, "Go on, scoot," again, then shut herself in, and I had time to try one more door, and if it hadn't opened, I would of busted something else for Lulu to subtract from my bicycle. But it did, and I was inside quick and trying to find a bolt before I even looked to see where I'd got to. I shot it home quiet, took a deep breath, and held it while the boots pounded past and the knob turned and rattled. I turned then, in case I was going to need a window in a hurry, and there sat Fred in bed with his jacket still buttoned up and his cap on and the covers pulled halfway up, and there beside him in the cider-colored light coming out of a shaded bed lamp with a pillow propped behind her back like she was expecting a breakfast tray sat a curly-haired blond dove. She had the covers pulled up as far as her waist, and she didn't have nothing on as far as I could notice, and there, pointing at me, was the first pair of bare lungs I ever seen—firm, middle-sized, and beautiful, glowing like something holy in a church picture—and I would of stood there for a long, long time, asking nothing more of life than permission to keep my eyes open, if it hadn't been for Fred who was holding a sixgun in both hands and aiming it right at me.

"It's me," I says, whispering. "Put that dang thing down."

Talking too loud, Fred says, "Don't move."

"Hush up," I says, and I slid sideways out of the line of fire, but the gun followed me.

"Is he a friend of yours?" the dove says in a sharp, whiny voice.

I couldn't pay her the attention she deserved, but I had to answer that just in case Fred might be in doubt or crazy or drunk. "Yes, indeed," I says. "My best friend on earth."

"Is that you, Jackson?" Fred says, like I was way down the street some place.

"Hush up," I says, whispering. "They just come by in the hall."

"Well, if he was *my* best friend," the dove says, "I'd sure do something about him so's he wouldn't be poking that gun around where it don't belong. Look at that," she says, pointing to a place on one of her lungs.

I was happy to oblige, though the bruise wasn't exactly my main point of interest. You'd think, with women carrying beautiful things like that around with them, they'd let them out in the open a little more often so's they could be seen and appreciated and thought over, but I'd been seventeen mortal years in Wyoming and hadn't laid eyes on any since my ma took hers away, which I can't even remember. It's a waste of time.

Fred had put the gun down in his lap now, which probably ain't the best idea, but I liked it better'n the other way, and a kind of strange admiration for him started dawning on me. I says, "Fred, what if your old man could see you now?"

"Where is he?" he says, reaching for the gun.

I got along the side of the bed so's the dove was partway between us. "I mean, I don't suppose you had a sum total of more than fifteen seconds of first-class temptation in your whole life, and you had it all in the last fifteen minutes, and you didn't last no longer'n a pie at a picnic," I says. "You're a drinking, gun-toting libertine, and you done it in record time."

"I can't see straight," Fred says.

"Don't forget you got to pay whether you take your clothes off or not," the dove says. "You took up my time."

While I had the chance, I slid the small window open further and took a look outside at the roof of the run-down saloon next door, maybe eight feet below. It wasn't too far to jump, but there probably wasn't nothing under that tar paper but hot air, and I didn't want to chance it. The day was getting dusky, but further along, at the back corner of the casino, I could see a strong-looking drainpipe.

Somebody commenced beating on the door. "Who's that in there?" a man says.

"It's me," the dove says in a high squeak. "Juliet."

"Who's with you?" the man hollers.

She took a look at Fred's gun beside her and says, "Nobody."

"Then what you locked for?"

"Oh, go away and don't bother me," she says.

And Fred took a shot at the door, just to make everything good and clear and aboveboard I guess, or maybe he done it by accident because he missed it by a foot and a half.

The dove let out a little screech, and I jumped to the door and give them three seconds to clear out of the hall (which is what I would of done in their place), then slid the bolt back, yanked it open, and ducked out. "Come on," I says, but not even really hoping Fred would follow. He was too heavy to carry and too wild to boss, so I had to leave him mostly on his own. I guessed right about the hall: nobody was there to shoot me, not even from back around the corner, and I ran for the door where the other dove had went through and tried it, but it was locked. I didn't have time to mess with the transom, and Fred wasn't fit to climb on anyway, so I rared back and kicked the bottom of my foot just above the knob. I had to do it three times before it whanged open.

I tried to shut it behind me, but it wouldn't go. And I was in some kind of plush-curtained place, dim-lighted, three times as big and sweet-smelling, kind of winy and roastbeefy like a dining room, and at first all I was interested in was the window closest to that drainpipe. But then I stopped cold because there at the far end, on a big kind of overgrown chair full of flowered cushions, raised hip-high off the floor and with a fringed roof on it sort of like a surrey, sat my old man in a blue silk robe, his fat bare gray-hairy chest sticking out and a stark-naked dove sprawled half in his lap.

I wasn't struck dead nor deaf nor dumb by it, but I got to admit I felt flabbergasted which is what some folks feel when they see a ghost: they go all weak and confused and don't feel up to much. It's sort of like in Chapter XII of WHAT A YOUNG BOY OUGHT TO KNOW where it tells what happens if a boy gets too many sex fits and commences to have his nerves ruint. "The bright boy that stood at the head of the class," says old Sylvanus, "is gradually losing his power to comprehend and retain his lessons. His memory fails him. His mind begins to lack grasp and grip. He cannot, as formerly, take hold and hold fast. Gradually he loses his place and drops back toward the foot of his class."

That's how I felt, but it didn't last but a few seconds. Then I started taking in the small table heaped up with dirty dishes and empty wine bottles and wadded napkins (which you wasn't supposed to do but put them back in napkin rings) and the clothes here and there on the floor (which you wasn't supposed to do but hang them up careful), including some bright-colored doves' clothes, and my old man's eyes bulging out at me, white all the way around.

And there I was at the foot of the class, only needing a stool and a dunce cap to finish me off, but I didn't feel like staying there. I walked toward them. It was only seven or eight steps, but by the time I come alongside the table and could of reached out and touched the dove's bare foot if I'd a mind to, I had got back to the head of the class again.

The dove, who'd been out in the hall before, says, "You're going to get in trouble."

I didn't pay her no mind, which just goes to show you how fast I was getting on to graduate, because she didn't have *nothing* on, and I was having to hang onto my wits in the middle of my first full view of the Grove of Venus.

My old man hadn't moved a stitch or a muscle, and now his eyes went back deeper into his head where they usually were. "Why ain't you home for supper?" he says.

"It don't look like there's any leftovers," I says, picking up a napkin and looking at the dried gravy on a plate.

He still had one arm around the dove. "Haven't you got to the part about breaking and entering in your extensive reading of the law?" he says. "Do you want to get me sued?"

"No, but I'm pretty well up on fornication in the Old Testament," I says, not knowing where the courage come from unless it was that whiskey.

"Don't you dare use that word to me," he says, scowling.

The dove says, "Is this your boy, Andy?"

"Never mind," he says.

Suddenly from behind me, Fred says, "Where's my old man?"

He was standing spraddle-legged, hanging onto a plush curtain with one hand, the gun pointed at the floor, and my old man and the dove come to life in a hurry: they was out of that cushiony love nest in nothing flat and dressing so fast I couldn't keep track of what I was missing.

"You said my old man was here," Fred says.

"I didn't either, I said what would you do if he was to—"

"Well, bring him on," Fred says. "This town ain't big enough for both of us."

My old man had his swallow-tail coat on over his silk robe and his hat on crooked and was leaning sideways against the love nest, like a steer scratching himself on a fence, trying to get his pants on.

"Come on, Fred," I says. "We got to go out the window."

"I don't want to go out no window," he says. "I'm sick."

I moved in toward him. "Then at least give me that gun."

"What gun?" he says, blinking around at everything like he expected to see one float past.

I reached for it, but he pulled it out of the way before I could catch aholt.

"Where is he?" Fred says. "He can't blame it onto me."

"Blame what?" I says.

"Evil is in the eye of the beholder," Fred says.

But there didn't seem like much in his eye but blurs, to judge by the way he was wiping at them and making little *Go away* motions with one hand. I checked my old man to see if he had himself pulled together yet, and he looked a sight, but it seemed like he'd got his dignity back on with his pants, even if he was barefooted. His face looked purple.

"What in the hell is Fred up to?" he says. "Is he drunk?"

"Is that you, Judge Holcomb?" Fred says, looking dumbstruck.

"Yes, put that gun down."

But I was kind of getting used to the gun waving around, and I had time to inspect the dove who'd put on bottoms but no tops. She was going into my dreams right then and there, permanent, like a gilt-edged investment to be drawed out and looked at now and then but never let go.

"Keep your eyes to yourself, Junior," my old man says, angry. "That does nothing but lead you into temptation and disease."

That was the first I heard about diseases, and I give the dove a careful once-over and says, "You got something wrong with you, miss? Allow me to recommend Celery Malt Compound the Great Nerve Builder."

"Nerve is right," the dove says. "I'm going to get Lulu."

"You ain't going anywhere," my old man says, holding her back. "Give me that gun, Fred."

"No, sir," Fred says, but not polite. His voice was getting louder. " 'Saying to a stock, Thou art my father; and to a stone, Thou hast brought me forth: for they have turned their back unto me, and not their face: but in the time of their trouble they will say, Arise, and save us.' "

I don't know whether he made it up or remembered it, him being such a great Bible-dodger, but he done it better'n his old man ever could of, and I was surprised.

My old man was beginning to get the message about Fred, and he cleared off a few steps around to the side of the love nest and commenced trying to get his shoes on without bending over or sitting down, which I could of told him it wasn't no use to try, and I stood there, growing older and older and wiser and wiser by the minute.

Then Lulu and Simon, both looking winded and mad, come between the curtains with a cowpoke-looking man behind them. She glanced over the whole scene with her hands on her big hips like we was kids caught pillow-fighting, and she finally settled on my old man. "Is something the matter, Judge?" she says, nice and sweet.

He was trying to wedge his feet into his shoes and looked like a man stomping out a campfire. "I thought privacy was the middle name of your business," he says. "I'm not accustomed to having my dinner interrupted by a gang of strangers."

He give me a meaning look when he says *strangers*, but Lulu didn't let him keep that notion around long enough to draw flies. "Why, I think it's fine a boy wants to eat and have fun with his pa," she says.

My old man went stony-faced then, thinking it over, and Lulu pointed at Fred. "There's that gun you was looking for, Simon, hanging right there in that boy's hand. Why don't you go get it?"

Simon turned gray and licked his thin lips and circled a little closer to Fred but out of reach, and Fred was sweeping his eyes around and blinking like he'd lost something.

"Go on," Lulu says. "It's yours, ain't it?"

Clanking shut his big belt buckle, my old man says, "I believe I'll be saying good evening now." He didn't have his shoes on right yet, nor no socks either, and the blue silk robe looked a little strange for a shirt, but he was set to go.

"Oh, don't do that," Lulu says. "The night ain't even old enough to vote, and you only had one supper. Now, Simon, take the gun away from that boy so's everybody can relax."

She made it sound easy, but it didn't look easy to me: Fred was acting kind of restless.

"Can't you quit talking about it?" Simon says. "I was just going to jump him and you spoilt it."

"I'll spoil you, you little nit, if you don't do your job," she says.

In a loud voice Fred says, " 'For though thou wash thee with nitre, and take thee much soap, yet thine iniquity is marked before me . . . A wild ass used to the wilderness, that snuffeth up the wind at her pleasure; in her occasion who can turn her away? All they that seek her will not weary themselves; in her month they will find her.' "

"Who you calling names?" Lulu says even louder, and the dove cringed backwards, and my old man edged over to the love nest like he was going to climb back in, and Simon and the cowpoke give her more elbow room, and I slipped sideways and had a look out the window which was partly open.

She'd hauled around right in front of Fred now with her feathers quivering, and he just stood there with his mouth open.

"I'm thirty inches between the eyes, and they feed me with a shovel," she hollers into his face. "I'm a potash-and-sulfur, Arizona strawberry mama from Wabash County with eleven tits and holes bored for more. Now give me that gol-danged gun." She took it away from him with one grab, then didn't pay no more attention to him. His eyes seemed to be coming into focus.

Simon come scurrying up behind Fred then and pinned his arms back, but the same thing happened to Simon that happened to me the last time I tried that on Fred: he don't like people pinning his arms. He don't mind losing a fight, but he can't stand feeling helpless. So I got the window all the way open while Simon was getting his nose bashed by one of Fred's elbows (he may be a preacher's son and no good with his fists, but he's got more elbows than a mop wringer) and then I yells out, "Come on, Fred!"

He come right at me and went right out the window past me even though I was halfway out myself and there wasn't no room for him to do it, and I thought he was going to dive straight through that roof next door and give the gents in the saloon something fresh to talk about. But he got aholt of the drainpipe somehow.

My old man says, "Come back here! Don't do that!"

But he wasn't figuring as fast as I was. Sitting on the sill with my legs in the great outdoors, I leaned back in for a second. "I'm the evidence, Pa," I says. "Without me, she can't prove nothing. All you got to do is deny everything."

He opened his mouth to give me hell, but I didn't wait for it. Fred had slipped and slithered far enough out of the way for me to get aboard, and the last thing I seen through the window was Lulu laughing, bent over and laughing, which wasn't quite what I'd expected.

9

⸻ • ⸻

Me and Fred sprang that drainpipe cockeyed getting down (which was going to be another chunk out of my Gent's Utah bicycle if my old man didn't bluff right), and we scrambled out of that neighborhood in a hurry. Fred was all sobered up and half sick by the time I helped him take a good dousing in the trough behind the hotel. It was almost dark out, and while he dried himself off on the roller towel, I did some calculating.

Whatever was going on at the Checker Casino was still going on, and no matter what time I got home now, my punishment was going to be the same: a whacking and a tongue-lashing from the housekeeper, worse food than usual for a day, and a showdown sooner or later with my old man. Mauger and Pinkus was up to something, and if we was ever going to find out what, one of us had to keep on spying. Fred was already rehearsing his excuses (which is what he called lies when *he* said them), and had his mind fixed on running the gauntlet between him and his bed: that gauntlet would be made up entirely of his old man, on both sides of the lane, through the house and up the stairs, and it'd be snatches of sermon and cuffs on the ear, each having to be explained away and apologized for after he swang, because Rev. Haskell didn't believe in corporal punishment.

So it was up to me. As soon as I was sure Fred was going to face up to his small-sized and familiar family Doom, I headed him in the right direction, stone sober now, and went back to the Checker Casino alone.

The trouble was, I didn't know what part of it to watch. The front door didn't seem like much use, and I couldn't see through any upstairs windows, and the back door by the privy seemed like it was too chancy for somebody like my old man: no telling who he might meet coming or going. And Pinkus had strolled right through the front, and probably Mauger too, like they was plain people with no shame, and maybe my old man didn't have no shame neither. And the root of the trouble was I didn't know what I was looking for.

While I hung around the back of the bank where I could see both ends of the casino from across the street, I felt like I'd been living my whole life in a fog and was just now realizing it was fog in front of my face, breaking up a little and letting me see for the first time that people had clear outlines, not a bunch of fuzz and blurs, and that things were going on—just a little ways off—I hadn't been able to see before. Why did my old man want to get himself up like a Shah or a Rajah and sit on a pile of cushions with a soiled dove? Was that what he done all day when court wasn't in session? It seemed like I'd been mooning around all my life, picking my ears with a straw, wandering around town or, lately, riding my bike through it, scratching at the edge of the prairie, playing games with Fred, thinking dirty thoughts without having no real girls to hook them on to, or just staring into space, getting a little older.

And I come to figure out, while I was standing there in the shadows with the shingles of the bank propping me up, that I never had much in my head and never had nothing good and exciting stretched out in front of me (nothing had ever been good for more'n an hour or two, and then it had petered out, and I'd have to find something different or else just whistle or whittle or putter—I couldn't even think up any interesting all-day daydreams), because my old man was too big and too powerful and too loud and too sure of himself and too sure of me. That was it, and that was what I should of told him up there in his love nest before he got his pants back on. Because now it might be too late. I might not have the nerve again, nor the whiskey to spruce it up.

The Checker Casino was getting noisier and fuller, at least downstairs, and every now and then somebody'd come out to the trough or the privy or next to it if it was occupied or off in the yard some place, but nobody I was watching for. And then I had an idea.

It was just like somebody taken me by the arm and led me across the street to the kind of wagon-track alley that went wobbling behind the casino, the saloon beyond, and the six or seven stores and sheds past that, and it was like he was saying, Now use your brains, son. If respectable people have to use the Checker Casino without muddying their good names, they can't use no front door or ordinary back door, and they sure ain't fit to climb drainpipes, so there's got to be a secret door, some way they can come and go without troubling their upright neighbors' noses. And if you was to install one of them, how would you do it?

Why, I says to myself, I'd put it in from next door or next door but one, and I'd make it so's my secret customers could get at it from the alley *or* the street, so they could take their pick depending on the time of day and who was looking.

And the man who was taking me across says, That's exactly right, son. You hit it right square on the bull's-eye.

And I passed the shadowy privy and some kind of storage shack behind the saloon and a heap of busted bottles and tin cans, and I was just locating myself a new spy post right in the middle of where I figured the secret entrance might be, when up ahead, almost at the next cross street where there was a little more light from something or other, I seen the outline of my old man and some other man I didn't recognize right away. They'd already come out the door before I found it.

Between me and them was about thirty yards of shadows full of ruts and shin-busters, and after I'd covered half the ground, I knew I couldn't get close enough to hear them without getting caught, so I held still and watched. I could make out the tunes of their voices but not the words; you can tell if somebody's riled or happy or worried or disgusted by how his voice rises or falls and whether he pitches it in his nose, his throat, or his chest, and by how fast or slow he goes. And my old man was both riled and scairt, going back and forth from one to the other: I'd heard him riled plenty of times, but never scairt. The man standing there with him was fidgety and stand-offish, like he didn't want to talk no more at all.

I'd seen so many people of all ages and shapes paying court to my old man—if I can say that meaning he was a judge and not a rich girl—it was a shock to see one putting him off. My old man actually went so far as to put his arm around the other man's shoulder—a thing I'd never seen nor felt him do to nobody nor to me—but the man shook him off and turned out of it, and as he did, the light come under his straight flat hatbrim, and I seen it was Mauger.

And right at the same time, while I was swallowing that fact like a lump, I heard somebody behind me. I'd been crouching by the corner of a shed, so all I had to do was slip around the edge and go flat, managing not to cut myself to slices on any sardine cans or busted bottles. And a few seconds later, almost near enough to touch, Pinkus come strutting by, trying to act tall, and it wasn't no soiled dove coming along behind him, aiming to get the rest of his greenbacks on her own time, but the Rev. Blenkensop Haskell, the Word made Flesh, in his black suit which was blacker than the shadows, saying, "Now, Samuel, be reasonable. Please be reasonable," and Pinkus sailing along ahead of him toward my old man and Mauger like reverends was beneath his dignity to notice.

They all had a short snappy palaver, then marched off, and by the time I got out to the corner of the buggy shop and could see them again, they was almost out to Main Street with Mauger and Pinkus in the lead and gaining ground fast. Out at the corner, my old man and Rev. Haskell just stopped and watched them go off, then had a little talk of their own, with the Rev. waving his hands or poking his palm with his forefinger like he was trying to stab it through and my old man just standing there stiff and motionless and big-bellied. They kept that up for about a minute, then my old man said something short, deep, and loud, turned around, and walked catty-cornered across Main Street out of sight. Rev. Haskell watched him longer'n I could, then hurried straight across the street into the dark in a different direction. When I got to the corner where they'd been, I couldn't see either of them no more.

I got on home then, going faster'n I could think, keeping ahead of my own thoughts so's I'd have something left to think about while I was laying in bed. The housekeeper was waiting for me in the kitchen, but I didn't try to sneak past her or climb up a tree and get through a window like in the stories: we *had* a tree, too, one of the best and biggest in town, a cottonwood eight feet tall but it was out in front and didn't reach nothing, and the only time I ever tried to climb it, I busted a branch and set it back five years.

I come in humble and apologized for missing supper, but she just set there on the bench on her side of the table with nothing in front of her and says, "Wash."

I give myself a rinse, a lick, and a promise at the kitchen pump, feeling her watching me while I bent over the sink, waiting for me to lie, but I wasn't going to lie. I didn't feel hungry neither, but I set down in front of my empty plate to get it over with.

"Go ahead," she says.

First I thought she meant say grace, and I was trying to remember how it went. I knew it started out "We thank Thee . . ." but I always got stuck there because it seemed dead foolish to call myself *We*, since I most always ate alone.

But she says, "Eat up."

Her streaked stringy hair was pulled back so tight in a bun, it was coming further and further apart, doing the splits so's her gray scalp showed. The end of her pointy nose was red, which always meant bad news. And then I realized it was a good thing I wasn't hungry because I wasn't going to get even cold stew. She'd thought up a new one. I started to get up and go to bed.

But she says, "You set there and eat."

I picked up my tin cup, made sure it was empty, then tilted it up and did some gulping sounds for her.

"Napkin," she says. "And mind your manners."

I took the napkin out of the ring, plopped it in my lap, picked up my spoon, and commenced scooping up air and putting it in my mouth like peas, maybe, or beans, just to please her and get it over with.

"Hold that spoon with the ends of your fingers," she says.

"What's wrong with getting a good grip on it?" I says. She was thin and hard-looking and dressed in dark clothes and not a trace of paint on her face, and she wasn't no dove, soiled or otherwise, not even a bird at all but some kind of homemade woman, put together out of old buggy harness and grandma clothes.

"Don't talk back," she says, "especially with your mouth full."

I kept it up a few more times, dinging my bare fork on the plate for a change, then I put it down and carefully rolled up my napkin and stuck it in the ring and pushed back my bench to get up.

"You haven't been excused," she says.

So I says it for her, and she says, "You may. At least till your father comes home." And when I was halfway into the dining room, she says, "Ain't you going to make up a story for me about where you been?"

"There's some stories that ladies must be spared," I says, and I was all the way gone upstairs before she could think up an answer.

But when I was all skinned down and under the covers and ready to think, my mind was too scratchy-eyed and tired. It didn't want to work for me. I tried to stare at the ceiling, but in a minute everything went shut and I was dreaming a whole jumble of dreams full of doves and money and horses and whiskey and books and Lulu and myself stuck in amongst it all, trying to figure out which of them things belonged to me and which was my old man's. And then he kept coming into it too, and I heard his voice barking and booming over the housekeeper's. And then I had a dream about that young cowboy on the pinto, only this time his pinto just stood there under him, meek and sweet as the boy Jesus, while my Gent's Utah bicycle bucked and shied and got its spokes tangled in sagebrush and finally threw me off and went wheeling away, end over end, from its front tire to its back tire like a nickel-plated tumbleweed. And I was left there with the cowboy, who looked just like me now, only smarter and tougher.

It was a long, long night, and when I woke up, I was tireder than before, but it turned out to be an even longer day, because my old man had disappeared and I had a brand-new one to worry about.

10

———— • ————

It happened like this. First, it was an ordinary morning with all the rattling and squeaking of wagons outside and the banging and clanking of the housekeeper inside (she treated the kitchen pump and the yard pump like they was fire alarms), and I knew I had about two more minutes of bed before I got roused out to "help," though she never let me finish doing nothing. It was always "Give me that broom, for landsakes," or "Don't you know how to redd up a sink yet?" or "Don't use so much lime with the slops, money don't grow on trees." I wished it did grow on trees, so she'd go off some place else to pick it.

But now for just those little minutes I had a chance to think, and I'm sorry to say my mind cooked up more sinful possibilities to explain what had happened last night than

Rev. Haskell could of drummed up for a backslider in a month of Sundays. I had my old man and Mauger and Pinkus in the midst of committing everything illegal or immoral I'd ever heard tell of, and I even left some blanks to fill in later in case I heard of any new way to sin or break the law. That sounds like I had a low opinion of my old man, but that's not true. It's just that I'd learned never to put anything past him, and now I had some mighty queer circumstances to try fitting him into. I even had myself in some of that scurry of daydreams, trying them on for size, and I was just fitting us all into posters saying WANTED FOR BANK ROBBERY (Pinkus looked best) and WANTED FOR MURDER (Mauger looked plumb natural) and WANTED FOR FORNICATION (Rev. Haskell took the cake on that one, but maybe just because he was forever talking about it), when the housekeeper poked the ceiling under me with a broom handle, which was her way of resurrecting the dead, namely me.

I lathered up for a shave (it was that time of the week) in my own basin, since I didn't want her watching me do it or saying, "Give me that razor," and by the time I'd dressed and gone downstairs to start choring, I had my day all planned out like one of the Revolutionary War campaigns I'd made up for Mauger's benefit in a history lesson: how I'd tell my old man I knew Mauger wasn't no lawyer and Pinkus wasn't no preacher and how I'd make him let me grow up right then and there and take my rightful place in his life (whatever that was) and how he'd own up to it all and tell me the truth and we'd be pardners and how I'd go find Fred then and let him in on it to be my sidekick, if he felt like it, since his old man was in on it too and had gone and spent all the Haskell family scruples in one spree.

But it didn't work out like that, none of it. In the first place, the housekeeper was crying, which was like hearing a prairie dog whistle "The Old Log Cabin in the Lane." It didn't stop her doing her chores or interfering with mine, but it was so impossible-looking—I'd of swore her tears was all locked up in a box under her bed—I couldn't think of nothing else. But then I had to, because before the pone and hash was ready to eat (it was never *fit* to eat, but I mean before it was ready cooked), Lawyer Shanklin, the one Mauger was supposed to be studying with, was at our back door with a set of papers, and the first-class confusion begun. It lasted all day, and I may not have things in the right order after a bit, because I was trying to keep track of too much at oncet.

First I got sent out of the room, then I got called back before I was even out and Lawyer Shanklin asked me what my birthday was, which started an argument with the housekeeper, who always had her own opinion about everything. And in the middle of all that, I come to find out, casual-like, that my old man's gone and both horses and the surrey too. And then Shanklin, who's a wispy, bare-faced bald man with a fringe of straight gray hair down over his ears and around the back of his head, told me to leave the room again, and I wouldn't do it.

"Where's my old man?" I says.

Now that she had something to fight about, the housekeeper had quit crying, and her and Shanklin herded me all the way into the parlor and made me set down on the horsehair sofa like a visitor (which turned out to be pretty near the case) while they both went back to the kitchen which was the only place in the house she felt comfortable in. By now I'd begun to soak up a few facts; my old man had been to see Shanklin before dawn with a whole set of papers already drawn up legal and "executed," which was what Shanklin kept saying, though it must not of meant what it sounded like. And my old man had Rev. Haskell and a soiled dove from the Checker along as witnesses. But I couldn't get much beyond that because the housekeeper kept wanting to know "What's going to happen to me? What's going to happen to me?" and Shanklin had to shove his words in edgewise.

Somebody knocked at the front door, and I beat the others to answering, but it was only some young pudgy-faced solemn-looking clerk from the bank with a straw hat set square on his head and a bushy red mustache, trying to look older'n he was, and he had some more papers for Shanklin who begun to get some surprises his own self.

It seems my old man had been to the bank too in the middle of the night, had hoorawed old Noah Flint, the president, out of bed and got him down there to open up the safe and transfer cash and stock and what-all to five or six different accounts and set up a couple of trust funds and convert this and endorse that, and I couldn't follow it, though Shanklin made the clerk take his hat off and sit down and describe some of it. But pretty soon the clerk shut his mouth up tight till his lower lip shot up under his mustache and disappeared. "That's private bank business," he says.

"But I'm ex-Judge Holcomb's lawyer," Shanklin says. "All signed, sealed, and delivered."

He might of been signed and delivered, but he sure wasn't sealed: he had his coat off and his vest unbuttoned now and his mouth open most of the time, and he was beginning to sweat, and I wasn't feeling so good myself. It was the first I'd heard my old man wasn't a judge no more, and if he wasn't a judge, then I wasn't a son of a judge. So what was I?

Shanklin was really looking worried by then. He'd come in acting like a undertaker who'd made all the necessary arrangements and wasn't going to let you see nothing that wasn't good for you, just the flowers and the velvet lining and the nice little painted smile, but the bottom had fallen out of the dang casket right in the middle of the first prayer, and now it wasn't even looking like the right corpse.

"You'll have to ask Mr. Flint about that," the clerk says in answer to about six questions in a row.

And anybody knows you can't get the time of day out of Flint—you can just barely see him head-on, him being skinny and got these dark eyes around on the sides of his face like a fish. But Shanklin was acting high and mighty, and nothing would do but we all had to go down to the bank.

"We've got to get this straightened out," Shanklin says, just like it wasn't him helped snarl it up in the first place. "Go put on a necktie, boy."

Meaning me. Well, I owned *two* neckties, but I wasn't about to put one on for Shanklin. I'd been sitting on that slick horsehair, trying to mind my own business (even though I couldn't tell where my business begun or ended), and I'd only had time to make up my mind about one thing: orders. I wasn't going to take no more. Not unless they happened to be the same orders I give myself. Not unless my old man had left some for me, and I wasn't even going to take them automatic. I says, "I'll be glad to go to the bank with you, but I'm going just like this." I had on blue-denim pants and an open-neck blue-denim shirt, and that was good enough.

"The bank isn't open for business yet," the clerk says. "Not until ten o'clock."

That took Shanklin's mind off neckties, and while he argued, the housekeeper tried to get me by the ear, but I stood up (which took it most out of her reach) and scowled right straight down at her. "You behave yourself," I says. "Grabbing people's ears! What the devil do you want to go grabbing people's ears for? You think they like it? If you feel like grabbing something, go on out in the kitchen where you belong and grab something to eat." That set her back on her heels for a few seconds, but I couldn't scrub off three ornery years that quick.

"You go up to your room and put on your Sunday suit," she says.

"Why don't we all have a shot of Celery Malt Compound instead?" I says. "Or better yet, why don't you go take a couple Dr. Worden's Female Pills for Weak Women, the Complexion, Beauty, Nerve, and Blood Maker?" because I'd seen them stuck back up in the spice cabinet behind the cinnamon sticks where she'd hid them. And I had her worried now: she hadn't heard me sass her more'n a couple words before. Then she had to go spoil it by starting to cry again. So I just shut up and went upstairs and got my ten dollars and small change and come back down and let events spread out in front of me by theirselves. But without no necktie on.

Shanklin had his coat back on and his vest buttoned up crooked, and the housekeeper was fetching her sunbonnet, and the clerk was shuffling around, looking over our parlor and living room like he was considering buying up the whole lot cheap at an auction, and he had his hat back on too (which anybody can tell you ain't mannerly).

"Mr. Flint will see *me*," Shanklin says to the clerk. "In case you don't know it, I have been elevated to the bench."

Which sounded painful till I come to find out he meant he was the judge now in my old man's place. And the clerk snapped to attention right away and got his hat back off while the housekeeper was tying hers on.

"The boy's upset and won't listen to reason," she says.

Shanklin scowled me over and says, "Maybe it's just as well. Mr. Flint ought to see just exactly what we've got on our hands."

I didn't have nothing on *my* hands, and when they started

out the front door I didn't have nothing on my head neither, though she tried to make me put on my black-felt crusher that had the brim turned up all the way around. But I sailed it off in the corner and went out bareheaded after them, and I wouldn't walk with nobody neither, and after a minute of huffing and clicking her tongue, the housekeeper went up beside Shanklin and left me straggling behind where I wanted to be, where I belonged. And when the procession come to Merle's Clothing Store, I ducked in for thirty seconds and bought me a buckskin felt sombrero for $3.25 that I'd been looking at for six months, and I had it on (tilted just right) before the housekeeper come trotting back to find me.

"Take that thing off," she says, but not sounding quite so sure of herself no more. "You trying to look like a cowboy?"

She said it like it should be my last wish in the world, and truth to tell, I didn't know *what* I wanted to look like, but it wasn't no lawyer and it wasn't no bank clerk nor no preacher nor no son of a judge. Nor no boy.

Shanklin was up ahead about ten yards, jawing something at me, and the housekeeper was keeping up her end of the snipping and sniping, and I come along for a few steps and then turned right into Arvine's Saddle Shop and bought me a pair of 19-inch black-calf opera cowboy boots I had all memorized for $4.75 while all three of them come to the front door to stare at me like I was a nitwit. Old Arvine wrapped up my other shoes, and when I stepped out the door I was two inches taller and a whole lot meaner-feeling, and I could see Shanklin trying to make up his mind about me. When he took off his Homburg to mop the top of his head, the worry crinkles was halfway up his scalp. After that, the housekeeper quit picking on me and seemed to get smaller.

Then we all come to the bank, me last, and just like the clerk had said, it wasn't open, but after some fussing back and forth through a chink of the front door that had a green shade pulled down it, we was let inside, and the clerk took us straight back through the gate and through two doors and into Flint's office (who people naturally called Skin behind his back), and there he sat behind a big oak desk stacked up with papers.

And then the confusion commenced in earnest, though Shanklin's favorite saying—"I just want to be sure everything's proper and aboveboard"—come chiming in at regular times like he was clocking himself. The housekeeper had gone dead quiet out of respect for banks, and when Shanklin asked her how old I was again, all she could do was turn pink and say, "If Mr. Flint will excuse me."

"What's she want to leave for?" Flint says. "She just got here."

"I believe she's embarrassed," Shanklin says.

"How old are you, boy?" Flint says.

"Seventeen," I says. "Old enough to know better."

"What you got on your head there?" Flint says, leaning back in his chair a little. "Didn't they teach you to take your hat off indoors."

"Be glad to oblige," I says, taking it off for practice. "Didn't they teach you to stand up when a lady enters the room?"

Flint leaned forward a little at that, lowering his sharp nose like he was considering giving me a jab with it. "You had better endeavor to be more civil," he says, "because I have been instructed to administer a trust in your name."

"Does that mean I have to trust you?" I says, feeling like I had a charge of whiskey in me, though I was talking back on the emptiest stomach in the West.

Then Flint and Shanklin begun talking money, and the clerk joined in for a bit till he was sent out of the room, and the figures was flying back and forth, and Shanklin was getting redder and madder, and he says, "I have been deceived and my client has been deceived, and as soon as my court gets into session, I mean to do something about it, you may rest assured."

"Which client?" Flint says. "Can't everybody be your client, or you'll have to hash yourself up and serve out portions if it comes to a court case."

And then the clerk come back in, bringing Mauger who's scowling even deeper than usual and who looks like he didn't make it to bed last night, maybe only as far as somebody's back porch.

Mauger give everybody one glance apiece, then fixed his flat black eyes on Shanklin. "Something go wrong?" he says.

"Let me do the talking now, Mr. Mauger," Shanklin says. "We don't want events getting too far ahead of us here." He turned to Flint. "It may interest you to know I have documents in my possession which directly conflict with and, indeed, contradict the pattern of trusts and holdings you've just outlined to me."

"Let's see what you got," Flint says, like it was a poker game.

"Where's the money?" Mauger says.

"Now, now, Mr. Mauger, as the senior partner in our law firm, I must insist on the right to speak for both of us on important occasions like this *in front of witnesses*," Shanklin says, leaning down on the last words and stuffing them as deep as he can into Mauger's head. He paused while Mauger just stood there, looking blank. Then he says, "Mr. Flint, I believe I will let those documents emerge to the light of day under legally controlled conditions. Who is your attorney now that Mr. Holcomb has absconded?"

"I will make a note of that last word," Flint says, searching around on his desk for a pen and not finding it.

"If I have correctly analyzed the information you have

given me," Shanklin says, "Mr. Holcomb is now in possession of upwards of thirty thousand dollars which rightfully belongs to my client."

"Which client?"

"Mr. Mauger."

"I thought he was your partner," Flint says.

"Under the law that doesn't prevent him from seeking my legal counsel," Shanklin says.

"You mean that old lard bucket snuck out with it?" Mauger says in a hollow level voice.

"And my counsel to you at the moment is to shut up," Shanklin says.

"In that case, get out of here, I'm a busy man," Flint says.

Piping up for the first time, the housekeeper says, "What's going to happen to me?"

And as long as she was going to do that, I figured I might's well get a piece of change out of it, so I says, "Where's my old man?"

"Suppose you tell us," Mauger says, coming close and looking mean. "You wasn't aiming to meet up with him anywhere, I don't suppose?"

For a minute I considered making up some geography for him, it being a familiar kind of game between us, but I was afraid Skin Flint and Shanklin might not be so dumb, so I says, "Well, if Rev. Haskell's right, we're going to meet in the Sweet By-and-By, but between now and then I ain't so sure."

"Clear out," Flint says.

"What do you know about Haskell, you little baggedy-britches numskull?" Mauger says, nice and quiet.

"Clear out," Flint says, "except the boy and the lady, and would you mind coming back in about fifteen minutes? I'll have this all straightened out, the clerk will show you a place you can set."

We all begun shuffling out the door then, with Shanklin trying to ride herd on Mauger, and the housekeeper trying to ride herd on me, and the clerk spreading his arms out behind us like a railroad conductor.

"I'll have a writ in here within the hour," Shanklin says. "When it comes to pulling fast ones, I'm no slouch myself."

"I'm already familiar with that fact," Flint says. "Good morning, gents."

The clerk showed us a couple of straight chairs next to a varnished picket fence, and the housekeeper set right down like she was glad to be doing something she knew how to do, but I wanted to keep my feet under me as long as Mauger was around, so I kept standing even when she yanked my shirttails.

Mauger come up close again and says, "Where is he?" And when I didn't answer right away, he says, "I'll have your hind end in a bundle for this. You and your old man went and connived it."

"Mr. Mauger, come outside," Shanklin says, almost screeching. The bank still wasn't open, and all the tellers was drinking in every word.

"I'm going to get what's rightfully mine," Mauger says.

"I sure hope so," I says.

The clerk had the front door partways open, trying to get Shanklin and Mauger to go through and at the same time trying to keep two other men from coming in. They were barged up against the outside of the door, jabbering at him, and one of them was Sheriff Worthy, who finally got his head through without wrecking his Stetson and hollers, "Come on out here, Shanklin."

Shanklin went then, but Mauger stayed behind, and he says to me, "That tutoring's going to go on just like before, boy."

"We'll see if it does," I says.

"Only the lessons is going to be a little harder now."

"You sit down and hold your tongue," the housekeeper says, yanking at me.

"That's good," I says. "I was afraid maybe you'd already taught me all you know."

"No," he says. "There's a couple little tricks and ideas here and there I figure I can add to your skull to take some of the numbness out."

Right then, I didn't know whether I was scairt of Mauger or not. I sure didn't want to be, but that dark bristly wide dished-in face didn't look too promising. I once found a burrow a little ways out on the prairie. It was too big for a prairie dog and too small for a badger, but when I put my nose down in it and took a whiff, I didn't want to find out what it was. It smelled like something that didn't want to be bothered much, and Mauger smelled just like it.

Sheriff Worthy had his head in the door again, and he says, "You, Holcomb, you come on out here a minute."

The housekeeper didn't want me to go, but the sheriff's got a bad temper even if he ain't got much else (my old man used to call him Worthless right to his face, though I never heard nobody else do it), so I went outside onto the boardwalk, and the clerk went and latched the door behind me, and Sheriff Worthy says, "Where's your old man?"

Which was getting to be a monotonous question. "I don't know," I says.

"The hell he don't," Mauger says.

Shanklin was trying to cut Mauger out of the herd and, I suppose, get him off to the law office where the mountains would be made plain and the crooked made straight, but the herd was getting a little bigger now, including a dude in a derby and a houndstooth vest and a lanky, worried-looking man in a brown business suit I'd seen a few times down around the railroad depot that somebody said was a road agent.

"When'd you see him last?" the sheriff says to me.

"Last night."

"Where?"

"Home," I says.

"What did he say?"

"Nothing."

"Why don't you leave me talk to him?" Mauger says. "Me and him's used to questions and answers. He's my star pupil. All's I got to do is give him a little drink and a little feed and a little pat on the back, and he'll sing like a bird."

"I'm asking the questions," the sheriff says. He wasn't very big, but he was chunky, and when he'd get mad he'd pull his neck in real short and hunch a little like he was about to run under something and heave it over.

The others backed off a bit, but not Mauger. He says, "Then start getting some better answers. I'm going to get my legal rights here or know the reason why."

"You're going to get your legal butt in a sling if you don't quit yelling at me," the sheriff says. "Old man Holcomb ain't here to protect you now."

"Calm down, gents," Shanklin says. "This isn't the time nor the place for a conference. If you'll just give me a couple days, I'll have this matter all cleared up fair and square, and you can all be getting on with your business just like always. The disappearance of Mr. Holcomb is regrettable, but it's only a temporary setback, nothing to worry about. As far as I know, all arrangements are fundamentally sound and still valid, Mr. Rose and Mr. Crosley"—nodding at the dude and the agent—"and you can start calling me Judge Shanklin right about now. My office hours will be posted, and I'll be glad to see you one at a time as soon as I get settled in. And

I think I ought to make it clear to you Mr. Mauger is my partner. My *law* partner."

The others was drinking this down like it was some new kind of medicine that maybe was going to be all right and maybe not.

"How'd all *this* happen?" the sheriff says in a low, worried voice.

"Why, we can't have any gap in the legal affairs of our fair city, can we?" Shanklin says. "If a judge chooses to leave us for good, no matter what the circumstances, we must have another judge. You wouldn't want lawless elements moving in where they've got no business, would you?"

"I want my money," Mauger said.

Shanklin lifted his hat and mopped the top of his head some more. "We must all be patient," he says. "In the long run, there's prosperity for all."

"Nobody's going to steal my money," Mauger says, looking right at me.

"Who stole what?" the sheriff says.

"The fact that you gents are here bright and early, knowing something went wrong, is a credit to you," Shanklin says. "It shows how keen and enterprising you are. But don't make the mistake of underestimating the others involved in this. The word has been out around the whole county for many hours now, and a number of important people have already consulted each other. Now you just cool off and wait your turn."

"It *is* my turn, goldang it," Mauger says. "I'm first."

"Who picked you for judge?" Crosley the railroad man says. "I reckon I'd have something to say about that."

"Well, now, it isn't too late to cast your ballot," Shanklin says, squinting his eyes and pinching his mouth tight. "Everybody with a vested interest is welcome to an opinion. Did you have somebody else in mind?"

"No, no, I'm sure it'll all work out," Crosley says, letting out steam and backing off fast.

"As long as nobody rocks the boat," Rose the dude says.

"Gents, I believe I may say without fear of contradiction, Business As Usual," Shanklin says.

Taking me by the arm, the sheriff says, "I want to have a little talk with you. Let's take a walk."

"Mr. Flint wants to see me," I says.

"Tell him to get in line," Mauger says. "I'm not going to wait around while my money goes rolling off north or south or east or west some place, God knows where, so you just better start talking fast, boy."

"I'll take care of this," the sheriff says. "You go peddle your papers."

The whole bunch of us was kind of drifting off sideways away from the bank and half into the street, and raising his voice, Shanklin says, "I think we'd best all quiet down a little, unless you want to start a public rally here."

"All I want to know is who's got Holcomb's power of attorney," Crosley says.

"I do," Shanklin says.

But I shoves in my two cents. "That ain't what Mr. Flint says."

"Flint don't know what he's talking about," Shanklin says.

"Come on, boy," the sheriff says. "Let's you and me go down to the jail a minute and have a cup of coffee."

"What's the Mayor's position on all this?" Rose the dude says. He's got some kind of little fake red flower in his buttonhole and a pearl stickpin.

"Go ask him," Shanklin says.

The sheriff was hauling me off a little ways, and Mauger come along and got me by the other arm.

"Leave go of him," the sheriff says.

"Don't tell me what to leave go of," Mauger says. "This

here kid's worth an awful lot of money to me, and I don't aim to let him get away."

The sheriff stopped and leaned close to Mauger, having to look up a little and stick his chin out. "There better not be no difference between what you aim to do and what I tell you to do. Now, leave go and git."

His voice going skinny and wobbly with the strain, Shanklin says, "Mauger, you dang bonehead, go on back to the office and wait for me."

"Too many people telling me what to do," Mauger says. "*I* know what to do, and I'm going to do it. I didn't spend all this time to get *told*."

It was a fine day out, I happened to notice—a nice high sun, no clouds, not hot yet—and people going about their business all around us, a few stopping to listen, the way they'll always do if there's loud talk and a scuffle, and Pinkus was among them, getting aholt of Shanklin by one lapel and saying, "What? What?" while Shanklin mumbled to him fast and tried to keep his own hat on. The whole bunch of us was across the street now, drifting and milling and gradually working our way toward the jail, which was right next to the courthouse.

Pinkus had on his usual crumpled-up brown suit, and his fat little mouth was hanging open. He shook Shanklin like he was trying to start a clock.

"You heard me tell you to leave go and git," the sheriff says. "That's my last warning."

"You ain't doing no such a thing," Mauger says, hanging onto me. "I've got my rights."

Reaching across me, the sheriff grabbed Mauger's sleeve and says, "I'm placing you under arrest."

"What's that?" Shanklin says.

They both kept aholt of me, and now the sheriff had Mauger, and we done a sort of ring-around-a-rosy there for a few seconds with Mauger cussing and the sheriff explaining about resisting arrest and me trying to keep my shirt from getting tore, and a merry time was had by all. I kept my feet out of the way so's nobody'd step on my new boots, and the sombrero was a good fit and stayed on, and if you asked me, Mauger didn't know no more about fighting than he knew about the War of 1812, which I had told him happened in 1822. The trouble was the sheriff didn't let his left hand know what his right hand was doing, and every time he give Mauger a yank or a twist, he give me something similar for leverage, and it was a rocky trip to the jailhouse.

By this time Shanklin was saying, "You can't do that, I forbid it," which anybody can tell you is the wrong thing to tell even a deputy, let alone a sheriff, specially when he's all riled up, and being a judge don't make no never-mind. You got to pour oil on troubled waters, my old man used to say, who never seemed to let trouble get too big a jump on him till that last night, but Shanklin hadn't learnt how to use his oil yet. All he could do was holler, and the sheriff was better at it than he was.

When we got to the jail, we could of sold tickets like circus people do when they finish a parade. And I got squeezed and scrambled through the door into the small front office.

While he was getting jammed through between Rose and Crosley, Shanklin says, "You can't do this to my client now, we've got important business to transact over in the courthouse. *Crucial* business, you idjit."

But the sheriff only had one idea in his head: he was aiming Mauger for a cell and dragging me along behind sort of absent-minded.

"What's his fine?" Shanklin says. "I'll pay it."

"I'll figure that out later," the sheriff says, all red in the face and his chin stuck out.

Mauger was still cussing and flailing and not getting no-where with it, and with the help of a stringbean-looking deputy with buck teeth the sheriff got him through the cell door, give him a boot in the rear end, and clanked the door shut and locked it.

Coming up close and talking in a kind of leaky whisper, Shanklin says, "You trying to wreck everything, sheriff? You don't know what's happened. Judge Holcomb left a bunch of papers with old Flint, and I've got to—"

"Everybody clear out!" the sheriff shouts. "Everybody!" The office was getting packed tight, and the sheriff started them all going backwards out the front door, pushing and stomping, till there was only the main bunch of us left and people gawking through the barred window.

Staying close, Shanklin says, "Use your head. We can't afford to have this young man out and Mauger in. There's *paper*work." He bumped me and got aholt of the front of my shirt.

Mauger had commenced hollering from his cell, and the sheriff says, "I don't give a *durn* what you want, Shanklin. Too much going on at once, things got to start happening one at a time. Everybody out!"

"In that case," Shanklin says, "I'll have to ask you to place Andrew Jackson Holcomb, Junior, under arrest for stealing Mr. Rose's pearl stickpin. I'm disappointed in you, my boy, since you can probably afford to buy one now."

And there it was, as big as life, sticking in my shirt above my breast pocket. Shanklin plucked it out and went *Tch, tch, tch* with his tongue.

"Will you make the identification, Mr. Rose?" Shanklin says.

"That's it all right," Rose says, fingering his foulard tie.

"All right, all right, if it'll make you happy," the sheriff says, hauling me back to the only other cell and boosting me in and letting the deputy clank and lock the door. "Now everybody out!"

And this time they almost did, but before the sheriff could get the door all the way swung shut on them, old Flint had pushed his way through, and Shanklin had come back with him, jawing away. The sheriff had cooled down a little, not having Mauger to wrassle with, and he give Flint room and acted respectful, just like the housekeeper done. I don't know why people want to be like that around bankers as long as they ain't asking for a loan, because what else can bankers do to them?—except maybe lock up the bank and not give nobody their money back. Maybe that's it.

"What's the meaning of this?" Flint says.

The sheriff explained, and Shanklin says, "I wasn't aware your assistance was required in jail matters, Mr. Flint."

"Why, obviously it is," Flint says. "Where's Mr. Rose? You, Rose, come on in here."

Rose squeezed in, holding his derby in both hands and nodding his head already like he knew all the answers was *yes.*

"I believe you've made a mistake," Flint says. "I see you're wearing my stickpin which I give to young Holcomb this morning as a keepsake. You must of mislaid your own and had a lapse of memory."

Rose fumbled the pin out of his tie and handed it over quick. "I do believe you're right, Mr. Flint."

Flint turned to the sheriff. "Now we cleared that up, you can turn the boy loose. I want to talk business with him, and I don't intend to do it between bars."

"Just a minute here," Shanklin says. "If Holcomb's getting out, I want my client out too. You had no call to put Mauger in there anyway. What's the charge?"

"Disturbing the peace," the sheriff says, his face getting flushed.

"What peace?" Shanklin says. "Whose peace? He didn't disturb *my* peace. Did he disturb the peace of any of you gents?"

"No, sir," Rose and Crosley says.

"He disturbed mine," the sheriff says.

"Well, in my capacity as judge I'm setting bail at one dollar," Shanklin says, "and in my capacity as Mr. Mauger's attorney, I'm paying it." He fished some silver out of his pocket and held it out.

"You ain't been swore in as judge yet," the sheriff says.

"And I doubt you will be," Flint says.

"And besides that, he was resisting arrest," the sheriff says. "And furthermore, I don't like him."

"I'm setting bail for resisting arrest at another dollar," Shanklin says, "and I herewith pay it." He fished out more silver. "And I don't recall any law that requires citizens to be likable around you, George Worthy, and if you want to keep that sheriff's badge, you better start laying up some sense against cold weather, because the north wind's going to blow, and if you get in its way it's going to blow you down." Shanklin wound up sounding like a preacher, with a high quaver in his voice.

The sheriff just stood there for a few seconds, looking mad. Then he took the two dollars and snapped his fingers at the deputy, who unlocked Mauger.

"Ain't a man in the world can do that to me and get away with it," Mauger says. "You're lucky I wasn't packing iron."

"If you had of been," the sheriff says, "you'd of been laying out there in the street with the hogs right now."

"Get out of here and wait for me in my office," Shanklin says.

Mauger shoved his way out, muttering and mumbling like he was practicing things to say next time.

"Now you let young Holcomb out of there," Flint says.

Changing to silky-sweet, Shanklin says, "I believe there's some question about the boy's complicity in his father's disappearance. Perhaps we shouldn't be too hasty in letting him out of our sight before we get this affair cleared up."

"Overnight he's become one of our leading citizens," Flint says.

Which sounded pretty peculiar coming out of a banker, especially with me sitting on a bare bench in a jail cell, wondering what was for breakfast and what's coming for dinner.

"He may have become a pore fatherless child overnight," Shanklin says, "but his legacy is under dispute, and if you doubt my word, you just try cashing in on some of it. I'm going to be in session in about five minutes."

"In session with who?" Flint says.

"Me, myself, and the court clerk," Shanklin says, pulling up stiff and trying to look taller.

"You talk too much for a judge," Flint says. "I think I'll go have a little talk with the Mayor."

"Don't forget the boy's underage," Shanklin says, blocking the doorway.

Flint smiled then, one of them fishy kind, like he was seeing me out of one eye and Shanklin out the other. "He'll age quickly under his new responsibilities. After all, he'll be handling an estate whose holdings include a third interest in my bank, twelve hundred acres of land right spang across the right-of-way of the R. M. & W. Railroad's ambitions, a first and second mortgage on the hotel and a half block of stores next to it, fifty-one percent of the stock in the Beulah Land Mining Company, mortgages on the Baptist and Congregational churches and their parsonages, the house he's been living in and all appurtenances thereto, a half interest in the

Checker Casino, and I do believe he becomes your landlord, Shanklin, unless you're figuring on moving into the judge's chambers and laying siege."

White in the face, Shanklin says, "We'll see about this."

"I'll skip over the bulk of the real estate and other assets too numerous to mention," Flint says.

The deputy come over and unlocked my door, opened it, and backed off, staring at me with his mouth open.

"All's I wanted to do was have a little talk with him," the sheriff says. "He wasn't under arrest."

"Oh, yes, I almost forgot," Flint says. "And one handsome pearl stickpin that's been in our family nigh onto five minutes." He motioned me out of my cell and pinned it into my shirt.

Shanklin clapped his hat on his head, went out the door, and scuttled off toward the courthouse.

"Anything I can do for you, Mr. Holcomb?" the sheriff says.

I fanned myself with my sombrero and tried to look Flint in both eyes at once, which ain't easy. "Can I afford something to eat?" I says.

11

————— ● —————

The first thing I done when I become rich was eat a stack of flapjacks, a cut of ham, and four cups of coffee over at the hotel, which I suppose I could of foreclosed on if I'd known how to do it. Flint watched me for a while and kept asking me questions about where I thought my old man might go if he had the whole country to pick from, what I wanted to be, whether my old man had ever mentioned this name or that name (a whole string of them), and if I was any good at arithmetic (which I ain't), but my mouth was so full most of the time, I took comfort in not talking, just shaking my head or nodding or shrugging. After a bit, he seemed to get tired of it and went back to the bank, telling me to put my food on the slate, which means you don't have to pay nothing. Not till later, anyways. If they can catch you.

I was supposed to meet him in the middle of the after-noon to get myself "straightened out," but I wasn't much looking forward to it, whatever he meant, because I wanted to be by myself and moon things over and think. I didn't feel like I had a home no more, and I couldn't picture staying in that place if the housekeeper was going to be there too. If I owned the house, like Flint said, I could turn her out, yet I didn't feel right about doing that neither, my old man hav-ing put up with her for three whole years. If I could of got her to go to Harvard Law School instead of me, I'd of done it, and she'd of graduated too, with honors, because I never seen such a one for strictness and for studying points of law (there's way more points of laws than there is laws, and it's like a great big-looking porcupine that's all quills and inside a little bitty rabbity-looking critter that wants to be left alone), at least around the house where she knew the proper place for everything and could prosecute a dislocation on the whatnot shelf blindfolded. And if she was only going to have *me* to summons and arraign and prosecute from now on, I didn't much like the dosage.

So while I finished eating and then strolled out into the street again, I begun making a list in my head of things to ask Flint about, such as Can I live at the hotel from now on? and Can I quit being tutored by the likes of Mauger and Pinkus? and Who says I have to go to church? and When can I buy me a horse? and What's a first or a second mort-gage? and Do I get to ride the railroad free? and Can I shut down the Baptist Church if I take a mind to? and Why did my old man run away?

By the time I got back to the front of Brady's Cigar Store, I begun to realize how little I knew about my life now. It was all just starting to form around me, and if I wasn't going to snap out of the fog and do some of my own thinking, all these loud fast-talking old men would get me stuck into some new kind of mess where I didn't have nothing to say about my rightful Destiny (which I didn't have no more idea about than a frog croaking at the moon, but I felt full of it anyway). And there, straight across the street, was the bank, which I owned one-third of, and catty-cornered was the Checker Casino, which I owned half of, though I didn't know which half.

The big question in my mind was what did my old man expect me to do with all that crazy property and stuff that Flint had run off on his list. And the only answer I could work up was he expected me to *be* somebody which meant wearing old men's clothes and setting in an office sober-faced and having discussions and maybe even hiring somebody to write down what I say (which would be a joke because I don't *know* what to say) and getting fat and becoming just like my old man. It scairt me. I heard myself saying *I'd ought to be able to do better'n that,* and that scairt me even more because people that tried to get ahead of my old man always wound up behind him. And the funny thing was I didn't want to be ahead of him *or* behind him but way off some place else, not safe and sound or high and dry but just different.

But here I was stuck with what was going to be a big stack of papers as bad as lawbooks, unless Shanklin managed to steal them off me, which I begun to hope maybe he would.

"Good morning, Mr. Holcomb," a voice says behind me.

And when I turned, I seen it was Brady himself, who wears his hair combed forward and plastered down on his baldpate in flat black curls and who never before said nothing to me but Get off them steps! or Can't you go loaf some place else, you kids? "Morning," I says.

"Have a cigar," he says, handing out a long skinny cheroot.

"Don't mind if I do," I says, sliding it into my shirt pocket next to the pearl stickpin. "I'll just keep it for brandy time, if that's all right." I don't know why I said that—cigars make me sick—but it seemed like I had to show him my old man wasn't the only one could handle a snifter.

"Why, sure, of course," he says, like it was the best idea he'd heard in a long long time. "Got some mighty fine Havanas just in from Chicago."

"What was they doing in Chicago?" I says, thinking maybe he was trying to catch me up on geography, like I done to Mauger.

But he didn't say nothing, just sort of faded off, smiling, back into his store where it seemed like maybe I was welcome now, not just to pick up an empty cigar box oncet in a while (unless Fred or somebody beat me to it) but to get me a full one. I begun to feel rich.

"Morning, Mr. Holcomb," says another voice.

"Morning," I says before I even turned to see who it was, which goes to show you how much most greetings is worth: already I was answering back like a dog been taught to sit up and speak. And it was old MacIsaac hanging out of his barbershop door on the other side of Plunkett's Dry Goods. He touched his forehead with a soapy razor in a kind of salute (a thing I wouldn't of done for pay), and I walked along as far as the barber pole to make sure it was really a smile on his face (I never seen one there before), and his customer sat up in the chair and broke a grin through a face full of lather and nodded at me too, whoever he was.

I nodded back and stepped down off the boardwalk to the street, looking around and feeling like maybe I was in the wrong town, and since my old man didn't seem to owe nobody money but Mauger, I figured all's I had to do was get rid of him, and I could run for mayor myself if I felt like it.

Will Judkins went by in his creaky old buckboard and dang near tipped his hat to me, but caught himself in time and just give me a nod and a big bacon-fat smirk like he was fixing to come calling on me. And when I crossed the street, getting some more practice walking in my high-heel boots, Arvine—who'd sold them to me—was out front of his saddle shop, nodding and chuckling like I'd just told him the hottest one he'd heard all month.

"Morning," he says. "I got just the saddle you're looking for. It's just been waiting for you."

Now, I didn't know I was looking for a saddle, but come to think about it, it didn't seem like such a bad idea. "I don't have nothing to go under it," I says.

"It don't matter which one you get first," Arvine says. "Bound to happen sooner or later, young man in your position."

While I thought it over (if you could call it thinking), I went down a couple doors to Merle's Clothing Store and picked out a pair of tight jeans and a red-and-white checked shirt with pearl buttons and a blue bandanna for around my neck, and Merle showed me how to tie the knot and even went and shoved the pearl stickpin through it. He wanted to help me change into the new things, but I done it by myself back in a corner. He wouldn't take my money, though I had just about enough, so I just chucked it all on the slate.

When I come out on the street again, I hardly knew myself, and when I tried to remember being anybody yesterday, all I could bring to mind was a raw boy that didn't know nothing about nothing.

Then right down my side of Main Street, weaving in and out of the hogs and little boys and heaps of manure, come the kid cowboy on his ornery pinto, the one who'd made me give up bicycles for good. He had to look at me twicet, then he says, "Well, well, what have we got here?"

I give him a long look to let him know I wasn't flinching, then started back toward the saddle shop, but I had to go and spoil it when one of my heels slipped between planks and made me twist my ankle.

The kid laughed. "Keep on your toes, boy," he says. "This world is full of wicked pitfalls."

"I see that skewbald jack rabbit ain't escaped from you yet," I says. "If she ever has a litter, save one for me, and I'll teach it to stop and go just like it was a real horse."

He had the pinto walking along beside me now. "Well, I guess they got to do *some*thing with the sons of judges," he says. "They might's well dress them up in doll clothes as anything else."

I stopped in front of Arvine's, and he got his pinto skewed around and more or less stopped, though it didn't seem to want all four feet on the ground at the same time. "That's a pretty good trick right there," I says. "What do you call that dance she's doing?"

He begun to scowl then. "I thought I learnt you a lesson last time," he says. "You want it all over again?"

"I don't remember learning nothing," I says, "except never to buy no Injun pony."

"If I didn't have nothing better to ride than a bye-cycle, I wouldn't be opening my big mouth so much," he says.

"Oh, I give that up," I says. "That was just for fun. Got me a fine bay mare now, just as sweet and smooth and steady. And fast? Why, she—"

"I got just what you're looking for," Arvine says behind me.

"Yeah," I says to the kid, "I was just going to get me a new saddle. I dang near wore out the old one."

He didn't say nothing to that, but went on scowling and looking mad, so I says, "Maybe I'll see you around, sonny," and followed Arvine into the shop.

And then Arvine commenced selling me an $18 saddle made of genuine oiled California skirting, a steel fork hide-covered tree, wool-lined skirts, a flower-stamped beaded-roll cantle, a beaded gullet, genuine California hair cinches, and leather-covered steel stirrups, which he explained item by item like I knew what he was talking about, with me all the time watching the kid out the window who was staying right there watching me. So I didn't have no choice but to buy it, or I mean put it on my slate, because I couldn't let the kid think I'd been lying. Which was my mistake: it must of weighed twenty pounds, and when I come out of the shop with it (I couldn't just leave it laying around in there if it belonged to me), I felt a little awkward.

"If you fancy having a race," the kid says, "now's as good a time as any." He didn't look too sure of himself and his horse didn't neither, shying and squirming like it'd just as soon run sideways or backwards as any other way.

And he was looking envious at my spang-new saddle too, which give me a little time to think: I could haul the saddle home to our stable and pretend my horse been stolen, but the housekeeper might be there, and she wouldn't stand for no lies around her and would have me all picked to pieces in a minute. So I says, "Sorry I can't oblige you, but she's over at Carter's Livery Stable getting shod."

"Well, when's she going to be done?" the kid says.

I hadn't thought that far ahead, and there I was toting a new saddle, so I couldn't very well say tomorrow, it wouldn't make sense, so I says, "Oh, sometime this afternoon."

"That suits me fine," he says.

Well, it didn't suit me at all, but there wasn't much I could say.

"What about right out west on Main Street?" he says.

"All right," I says and stood there waiting for him to go

away. But he didn't. He kept staring me over, up, down, and around.

"If you don't beat all," he says, shaking his head.

"I'll beat you anyways." I kept my eyes on his till they started watering.

"Where'd you get that hat?" he says. "You look like something got chased out of Mexico for scaring the dogs."

He was wearing a greasy old Stetson. "If you don't know a good sombrero when you see one, more's the pity," I says. "No law says everybody has to go around looking like a junior cowpoke hunting a sugar-tit." I seen from the look on his face then, I was going to have to fight him if I kept that up, and though I'd sooner fight him than race him, I didn't want to do neither. So I remembered my new position in the community and says, "I'll buy you a drink if it won't ruin you with the Band of Hope. I wouldn't want them to take your sash away from you."

He looked surprised. "You got some place'll serve you?" he says.

"Didn't you hear?" I says. "I own half the Checker Casino, and I reckon that's good enough for a drink." I didn't know for sure whether it was or not, but I'd sure a lot rather tangle with Lulu than a horse race before I got a chance to practice up. Or at least buy something of my own to put under the saddle.

His mouth come open and stayed open. "Half the Checker?" he says.

"You heard me, come on," I says, heaving the saddle up on my shoulder and starting down the block past the hardware store and the Sunflower Café, and a couple people I didn't know give me nods and good mornings, and I begun to get some idea how my old man must of felt for years and years, with folks spreading butter on him and putting down dishes of cream for him and letting him see their smiling teeth all the way back to the molars. You have that happening long enough, and you begin to think there's nothing in the world to worry about. Then the first thing you know, you have to run out of town in the middle of the night, and somebody else is licking up the cream.

The kid come along on horseback, having to wait at the bank corner for a couple of wagons to go by, and we both crossed over to the rail in front of the Checker Casino where he dismounted and tied that pony's reins in a double knot.

"You want me to get a spike maul so's you can nail her down?" I says.

"She's a mite skittish," he says. "But she's a good horse. You there, Taffy, simmer down! She ain't used to all these city goings-on. She's used to having thing's hold still unless they got horns on them."

I tried to act calm by them swinging doors, but to tell the truth, I didn't like the feel of having to go in there and boss my way through to a drink I didn't even want much. Seemed like I'd spent the whole day arguing or listening to other people do it, and all I wanted was to set down and give my jaw a rest and listen to the blessed sound of people's brains and tempers settling back into place in the bottom of their heads and bellies. Yesterday I'd been wishing for excitement, but I felt like I'd had a heap too much of it, and here I was going through the swinging doors apurpose to show off in front of a kid whose opinions I shouldn't give a durn about and without even Fred to see me do it.

And then suddenly it come to mind my old man might not like what I was doing, and for a couple seconds I felt worried, same as if I was liable to hear him hollering, "Jackson! Get on home!" any minute or "Get on up to the office and crack those lawbooks!" And truth to tell, I *could* hear him inside my head which is a sneaky way old men got to boss you even when they're not looking. I had to force myself through the swinging doors, and I couldn't leave the saddle outside or somebody'd swipe it sure, so I went butting in sideways with it, looking for a place to stash it.

Old men leave their voices laying around every place, saying Don't do this and Don't do that and Find out what Junior's doing and tell him to stop. All that advice and all them rules—they're as careless about passing them out or dropping them off as they are spitting or tossing away cigar butts. What are old men good for if once they lay down the law all they do is run off? Run off some place where they don't have to obey nobody their own selves? Fathers sure take up a lot of time, even when they ain't there. So I quit listening.

There wasn't but a half dozen people in the bar, but one of them was Pinkus, who had himself back in the same spot he'd been last evening. I led the way up to the near end and let the saddle plop to the floor.

The tall fat bartender with garters on the sleeves of his striped shirt braced his arms and leaned over at us. "We don't take nothing in trade, boys," he says.

"Are you new here?" I says.

"I ain't as new to tending bar as you are to walking on your hind legs, boy," he says. "Now you pick up that saddle and turn around and go put it back where you found it."

"My name's Jackson Holcomb," I says, "and I'd hate to have to fire an old-timer like you for driving off trade. I'd like you to meet a thirsty friend of mine, Mr.—"

"Lassiter," the kid says.

"—Mr. Lassiter who's been out collecting dust in his throat on the lone prairie, and we'd like a couple of whiskeys," I says.

The bartender just stood there staring at us, not doing nothing, and a soiled dove, a redhead who looked like one of the team from up on the third floor, come wandering over with her hands on her dished-in waist. She had on a short pink frilly dress, and whoever made it must of run out of material around the chest. "It's him, all right," she says. "You want me to get Lulu?"

"Yep," the bartender says, still not moving.

"You fixing to do some riding in here?" the dove says, giggling. "Most does it bareback."

I seen Pinkus edging down the bar toward us, like he was trying to make up his mind what to do. "Why, I thought the Checker Casino was a home away from home," I says. "I brung my friend in here to wet him down a little, and I hate to keep him waiting."

"Better get Mr. Rose too," Pinkus says. "I think he'd like to see this."

"Okeydoke," the dove says, skipping off through a side door.

"Morning, Pinkus," I says. "You come here to testify?"

"*Mr.* Pinkus," he says.

"How about Reverend Pinkus?" I says. "You might's well go whole hog, it don't cost any more'n porkchops."

His round face turned pinker and damper. "You better start saving up some good will, boy," he says. "You're going to need it."

"I reckon I'll supply my own needs from here on out," I says. "But if I can help *you*, just let me know. I'm ready to do the Christian thing for you. I'll even help you extract Jesus from the Book of Exodus if you want me to."

Lulu come steaming through the side door at the far end of the bar, and I reached down and got hold of my saddle horn in case she was going to storm us out. But she slowed down after she got past Pinkus and just stood there looking at me. She had on some kind of a long green robe with orange dragons on it as big as a tent.

"This place is getting so full of Holcombs, I'm going to have to turn the cat loose," she says. "Every time I turn around, there's another one. Now you just trot on out and play cowboy, or whatever that is you're doing."

"I come to look over my fifty percent," I says. "Is this it down here or do I have to go upstairs?"

"You haven't even got fifty percent of your own brains," she says, but she didn't sound too sure of herself.

"What was the last head count of Holcombs?" I says, getting a wild idea. "Is my old man upstairs some place?"

The few people at the bar were clearing away from Lulu, including Pinkus who was drifting off behind her, like she was getting ready to throw down on me, and truth to tell, she could of been wearing a gunbelt under her robe and even had a friend along under there to draw for her. She says, "One Holcomb seems like ten. The Judge is halfway to Chicago, if you ask me."

"My friend Mr. Lassiter and me come in for a drink a while back," I says, "and I hope to tell you, you got a slow bartender."

"Both too young," Lulu says.

"I figured being part owner's aged me," I says.

Pinkus says, "Judge Shanklin will have that taken care of before noon."

"They can split a quart of beer," Lulu says to the bartender, and he thumped it out on the bar with two steins and says, "That'll be one dollar."

"Put it on the slate," I says.

"If I was you, I wouldn't give credit to an orphan in a storm," Pinkus says. "Food and sympathy maybe but not credit."

Lulu hesitated, then says to the bartender, "Go ahead."

And I handed a stein back to the kid and filled us both up with a good head on it and got set for the second beer of my life. I lifted it up all around. "Here's to all the sinners and soiled doves who been trying to get to Hell through the Checker Casino and ain't made it yet," I says.

Simon come out of the side door and stood looking at the far end of the bar, and then Rose the dude come out too with his derby on, and the temperature in the place went down a bit.

"Well, if you ain't a chip off the old butcher block," Lulu says. "All's you need to do is gain about a hundred pounds and turn gray, and nobody'll miss the Judge at all."

"He's not the Judge no more," Pinkus says. "Shanklin is."

Lulu clapped her fat hands together like she was calling a bunch of kids to supper and says, "Well, I'd say Shanklin's got a ways to go yet. I'm afraid I'm going to have to buy everybody a drink, just for the hell of it."

Rose come up close behind her at the bar. "No house drinks," he says.

Lulu give a kind of jerk and stared at him. "What's that?"

"I said no house drinks till I get a full accounting," Rose says. "You got a short memory."

"I got a short memory for shorties like you," Lulu says, and a couple of doves giggled back among the tables. "I said *I'm* buying."

"Well, that's all right then," Rose says, scowling at me. "You can just hand over that stickpin now, young man." He held out his palm.

I wasn't feeling any too rich any more, but I didn't exactly know what to do about it. Lassiter hadn't even tasted his beer yet, but was just looking all around with his eyes wide open like he'd turned into his own horse, and when I took a sip of mine, I wished I hadn't neither. My old man always used to say, When you don't know what's going on, just shut up and you might learn something. So I give it a try.

Simon come up alongside Rose, and Rose says, "My stickpin, please."

The bartender was setting up drinks, pouring and clinking and popping beer corks, and Lulu says, "Well, it's a great day for getting your own back, I guess. I don't believe I ever seen so many people who didn't want nothing but their rightful share. The only trouble is, it looks like somebody already et the pie they's fighting over."

"You'll find out," Pinkus says.

"You want to lick the pan there, Reverend?" Lulu says. "You might be able to tell what kind of pie it *was*."

"I'm waiting, young man," Rose says.

Simon edged off away from him out in the open toward the tables and made a little loosening-up move around the handle of his sixgun.

And here I was in trouble again, without even half trying. It didn't seem to take no effort at all on my part, and I could get myself in fixes worse'n the kind you dream up all night when you got the collywobbles. But I kept still for a while yet.

"You, Simon!" Lulu hollers like she was calling hogs, though she wasn't but five feet away from him. "Go on back to sleep and behave yourself."

"I'm working for Mr. Rose," Simon says.

"You don't know who you're working for," she says. "Or what. Or why. Or nothing, not even *if*."

Rose still had his palm out. "I'll take that stickpin now."

"Mr. Flint give me that," I says. "Been in his family for years, and I'd hate to have to tell him you took it off me."

Simon took his gun out sort of absent-minded, and Rose says, "You know very well it's mine, and you know very well

• 1 1 5 •

how it came into your possession: Shanklin stuck it in your shirt."

I fingered the pearl in my bandanna, keeping one eye on Simon. "How much is it worth to you, Mr. Rose?" I says.

"I wouldn't take fifty dollars for it," Rose says, "if it's any of your business."

"Why, Mr. Rose," I says, "do you realize you're accusing Shanklin of being an accessory to a felony in front of witnesses? You can get in a whole lot of trouble doing something like that, if he should happen to be the kind that likes to sue."

"All he did was borrow it for a joke," Rose says, turning rosy. "And now the joke's over."

Simon clicked back the hammer. "Right now," he says.

The bartender had slowed down his drink-making, and Lulu was just opening her mouth to let out a piece of her mind, and I pulled out the stickpin with my free hand and took a step closer to Rose, but at the same time come close enough to Lulu to stick it through the top folds of her robe where it crossed over her big chest, which I done, spilling some beer on my boots and her slippers. I says, "Miss Lulu, I just decided to pass this little keepsake on to you in memory of my first evening in your establishment and my old man's last."

"Why, ain't that sweet," Lulu says, adjusting it and breathing on it and giving it a quick polish with her sleeve.

"It's not his to give away," Rose says. "Hand it over."

Half turning, Lulu could see Simon's gun had kind of drifted off me and over at her, and she says, "Watch where you're aiming that thing, or I'll take it away from you and shove it in one ear and out the other and give that spittoon you call your head the reaming-out it's been asking for."

Simon turned the gun away and got it pointing more or

less at me, and Rose says, "I'm not going to ask again." He had his palm out to Lulu now.

And she says, "That's good, because it's sure getting tiresome hearing you go on about it, Rosie."

The kid, who'd been halfway behind, stepped up even with me, holding his beer, and he says to Simon, "Are you pointing that at me?"

"Keep still," Simon says, only half looking at him.

"You got no call to do that," the kid says.

Raising his voice, Rose says, "That's my luck charm, Lulu, and you're not going to steal my luck. You already stole enough or I miss my guess. When I get through with those account books—"

"Who you calling a thief, you little yellow-faced deckshaver, you?" Lulu hollers. "You ain't nothing but a brokendown card mechanic who been run out of every clean game east of Abilene. You say something like that again, and I'll peel off that little mustache of yours and stick it back where it come from."

"That's pretty good, coming from you," Rose says. "If there's anybody can cuss better than a hustler, it's a madam."

And Pinkus pipes up from down the bar, "Don't get het up over nothing," he says.

Looking fit to bust, Lulu says, "Tie that little bull outside! There's going to be raw meat for the poor folks tonight! I'm going to pluck me a rose and wear it between my teeth!"

And while she was hollering on like that, taking up most of the attention, the kid went forward another step and threw his beer in Simon's face, stein and all, and wrenched the gun away with the other hand. And then, just as I was getting to enjoy the spectacle of Simon wiping himself off and rubbing the bunged-up place on his forehead, Pinkus pulled a little revolver from inside his vest and says, "Hold it!" in a high voice.

But some kind of a scroungy old man behind him, with a beard half the color of eating tobacco and half gray, wearing fringed buckskin like some old liar in a medicine show, reached around in front of Pinkus and just plain took the gun away from him, like maybe he wanted to borry it to look at for a minute, and the old man says to Pinkus, "Son, if you want to get yourself shot, the first thing you got to do— howdy, there, Kid," he says to Lassiter, giving him a little wave of the pistol butt "—is make sure there ain't somebody in back of you who don't want to be in the line of fire when you get yourself killed."

"Hello, Greasy," the kid says.

Everybody was standing dead still and trying to look two ways at oncet, and the old man says, "Now the Kid there ain't killed nobody yet, far as I know, but it prob'ly won't be too long and it sure as hell won't be too much trouble for him to do it because I taught him how to shoot myself, didn't I, Kid?"

"No," the kid says.

"Well, that's just modesty," the old man says. "He don't want to brag."

Pinkus tried to grab his gun back, but the old man give him an elbow right under his outstretched arm, and though I didn't hear no ribs crack, Pinkus let out a first-class thud and a grunt, and kept his hands to himself.

"Well, what do you figure on doing now, Kid?" the old man says. "Haven't had the drop on a whole barful in many a moon."

"I believe we was about to get a free drink," the kid says.

"I seem to recollect something about that too," the old

man says. "And I wouldn't want to interfere with a friendly occasion, specially when it's the work of a lady."

"I didn't see you," the kid says, sounding apologetic. He was keeping his gun on Simon and nobody else.

The old man walked away from Pinkus, holding the gun by the stubby barrel and scratching himself under the beard with the butt. "Son, that's one of the laws of nature. Old-timers is invisible to the naked eye unless they speak up." He paused at an empty table. "And I didn't know but what you was still mad at me. Madam," he says to Lulu, "do I have your permission to seat myself so's I can enjoy your hospitality to the limit?"

"Go ahead, Greasy," she says. "There ain't no limit front, back, or upstairs."

"I wasn't mad," the kid says.

"I've had about enough of this," Rose says, and he turns and stomps off toward the back, and I have to give him credit: he didn't look at the kid's gun. He stopped way back at the side door and says, "There'll be some changes around here, believe me," and he ducked out a little too fast to be dignified.

Lulu turned on Simon, who was standing there, blinking and dripping, and she says, "Simon, if you want to get ahead in this here world, what you want to do is start charging rent for that sixgun. At fifty cents an hour you could make yourself a heap, if somebody don't shoot you with it first."

Simon looked from the kid to me to the old man and says, "I got a long memory," and started after Rose.

"Then you can tell your grandchildren about the day you didn't get shot by Kid Lassiter and Greasy Brown," the old man says.

"I didn't draw that gun in anger," Pinkus says, still planted in the same spot where he'd been. "I was merely trying to prevent serious injury, and when two young hotheads take to struggling over a gun and throwing beer around, I draw the line. Now give it back, the trouble's over." He held out his hand to the old man, who was ten feet away, but neither of them moved.

"What's a preacher want with a gun?" I says.

"A preacher!" Lulu let out a short loud laugh. "Are you a preacher?"

"That's my business," Pinkus says, taking a step or two toward the old man, but hesitating. "Nobody takes my gun away from me."

"Why, somebody just did, Pinkie," Lulu says. "So don't tell no fibs."

Raising his voice toward the old man, Pinkus says, "I'm waiting."

"Well, pull up a chair and set down while you're at it," the old man says, "because it's apt to be quite a spell."

His lips looking white and jittery, Pinkus turned to the Kid and says, "Is this a holdup?"

The Kid aimed the sixgun at the floor. "I don't think so," he says. "Is it, Greasy?"

"No," Greasy says.

"I'm being held up and robbed of a .32 pistol at gunpoint," Pinkus says. "I call you to witness, Miss Lulu, and I intend to report this to the sheriff at once."

"I'll be a witness all right," Lulu says, "and I'll tell everybody on this side of town just what I seen because there's no use denying folks a good laugh."

"We're just keeping the peace," Greasy says. "Don't neither of these guns belong to us, but we didn't pull them in the first place."

Pinkus says, "That doesn't alter the fact that—"

"And when we leave," Greasy says, "they'll stay behind in

possession of the bartender who is the *slowest* man at setting up a house drink I ever did see."

Changing from pink to red, Pinkus says, "You're making a mistake, Lulu. Things are going to change around here, and there's plenty more canary-keepers where you come from."

"Why, you overstuffed knock-kneed sawed-off wet-chinned beady-eyed unwashed claim-jumping hairy-eared lard-bellied freeloading slewfooted slop-headed nickel-nursing wart!" Lulu says. "Are you threatening me?"

Pinkus looked sorry he'd brung up the subject, and he backed off a little toward the side door. "I just don't like to be crossed," he says.

"Crossed!" Lulu says. "Why, you don't know what crossing is, and you a preacher! You think Jesus had it bad, you just threaten me some more, and I'll nail you up in places you never dreamt of. I'll skin you and stretch you and salt you down and wear you for a nightshirt, which is the closest you'll ever get to me or any girl of mine again. Now get out of here."

Pinkus backed up further toward the side door, brushing at his coatsleeves like he'd just fallen off his horse. "You don't own enough of this place any more to throw anybody out," he says, but quiet and sort of to himself.

"You scat," Lulu says.

Around the edge of the door, Pinkus says, "All right, it's the sheriff."

When he was gone, Lulu says, "Well, that's one less mouth to feed," and she supervised the passing out of free drinks (more beer for me and the Kid), and when we'd toasted her (Greasy saying, "Bang it, Lulu, bang it," but very polite), Lulu says, "Okay, now, everybody out. This place is closed till somebody figures out who owns it legal."

And with the help of the bartender she trooped us all out

the front door—the couple of other customers acting meek and quiet—and the Kid and Greasy handed over the guns just like he'd said, and that's how I come to be standing out on the boardwalk with a twenty-pound saddle and no place to go.

12

———— • ————

My old man used to have a lot of sayings (most of them wasn't necessarily his because I heard other people say them too, unless they learnt them from him) such as *There's no road without a turning* and *There's no use crying over spilt liquor* and *There's no place like home,* and there outside the Checker Casino it come to me how true all of them was, even though my old man used to say them too loud and kind of laugh like they *wasn't* true. Well, I had come to a turning in the road at long last after clomping along straight as a string for seventeen years, and I wasn't crying over my old man because he was gone like brandy out of a snifter, and I sure wasn't going home: there wasn't no place like it, and that was just fine with me. The fewer places like home I could find, the better I'd feel.

Greasy Brown was the rumpledest-looking man I ever seen, his buckskin all smudged and his beard tangled and his old straw Stetson with its crown broke and his boots lopsided, but somehow or other he looked dignified. And I think it was maybe because he always seemed to know what he was doing, even when he didn't. When he looked up and down the street, like he done now, he seemed to know right where he was at, and when he talked to the Kid or me or dropped a word to a stranger, like he done now, he seemed to know exactly who he was talking to and who was doing the talking. It wasn't so much what he said, but how.

"It ain't even noon yet," he says, looking at the sun, "but I feel like I already earned my dollar."

The Kid says, "Greasy, if you keep trying to settle other people's quarrels, you better start packing a gun."

"What for?" Greasy says. "Look at it logical. There's mighty few who'll shoot an unarmed man, so I got both hands free and a man with a gun's only got one, if that many, and just as soon's I take it away from him, why, I've got the only gun, so there you are."

"Supposing he's got two guns," I says.

Greasy give me a slit-eyed look. "Why, who'd want to hold two guns on a weak and washy wrung-out old man, sonny boy?"

The Kid let out a high cackle, and his cowpony dang near uprooted the railing. "What if he ain't got no gun at all?" he says.

Greasy smoothed the front of his mustache around with one hand like he was trying to find his mouth. "Then you don't have to pay no attention to him," he says. "This world is full of two kind of people: them with guns and them without, and them with guns think they know the difference. Well, they don't."

"This world's full of two kind of people: drunk and sober," the Kid says. "And the sober ones think they can tell the difference."

"Well, they can't," Greasy says, and his beard rustled and shifted around his mouth, and he let out a sound like *Haw*.

"Two other kind of people," I says. "Them that spill their beer and them that drink it."

Greasy says, "You two come into the Checker like you was fixing to use it for kindling wood."

"I been challenged to a race," the Kid says, "only he ain't got a horse."

"I told you it was getting shod," I says. "What you think I got this here saddle for?"

"I think you got it to put on your bye-cycle," the Kid says.

Raising his voice, Greasy says, "There's two kind of people in this world: men and boys. And the boys always think they can tell the difference."

"Well, they can't," the Kid says.

"Maybe they can't, but I can," I says. "And if there's only men and boys, which kind are them soiled doves in there?"

"I see I have fallen among quarrelsome pardners," Greasy says. "What day of the week is it?" He looked around like he expected to see it wrote on the wall.

"There's two kind of people in the world," I says. "Them that knows what day it is, and them that don't. It's Friday."

"If you'd used up as many Fridays as I have, boy," Greasy says, "you wouldn't much care whether they was Sundays or Tuesdays. If you'd seen as many sunrises and high noons and sunsets, with the sun going down the gullet of the West like a raw egg yolk in a prairie oyster, you wouldn't keep close track neither. Well, now let's see here," he says, gawking all around at the dusty street and the wagons and the horses and the people and the boardwalk and the hogs and the tin cans and a couple of stray head of cattle come to town for a look-see and then at the Kid and me. "What do you reckon we ought to do?"

He put it like a serious question, but I couldn't think of no answer right off, and the Kid says, "How about some grub?"

Greasy made some kind of a face because all his whiskers come in toward his nose for a second, and he says, "No use spoiling a beautiful week by putting a bunch of trash in our stomachs, is there? There's been enough sowbelly and beans pass through me since spring to kill off the U.S. Cavalry, and I ain't about to empty my poke for what I'd just as leave throw away. Now let's see: what did the Lord do on the fifth day?"

I knew that one, so I says, "He created the beasts of the field and the birds of the air and the fish of the sea and all things that creepeth and crawleth on the earth."

Greasy lifted up his hat like he was letting a little air under, and his gray hair come flapping down over his ears. "Well, if it's good enough for the Lord, it's good enough for me, so all we got to do is follow the divine plan: first we got to act like beasts, then we got to fly through the air, then go swimming, and then maybe by sundown we'll see whether we're any good at creeping and crawling. How does that sound?"

It sounded just fine to me, and I'd of done all five right then and there if somebody'd showed me how, but the Kid says, "You got to be back by Sunday this time, Greasy, or Rafferty's going to lay you off sure."

"It's a long time till Sunday," Greasy says, "and we got the Lord's work to do. What all did He do on the sixth day?"

"He made Adam," I says.

"How about Eve?" Greasy says. "That's more in my line."

"I don't exactly recollect," I says, "except Adam was asleep when it happened." I'd made up too many Bible stories of my own for Pinkus, and sometimes I couldn't remember which was mine and which was the Lord's.

Greasy let fly a squirt of tobacco juice that was the straightest, furthest, and fastest spit I ever seen, and I ain't seen better since: it went right on a line out near halfway in the street past the Kid's pinto, who shied and jerked her nose up. "Well, I see first off it's my duty to dye-rect and judge this here race between you two so's you'll quit trying to nip each other's flanks and we can have a little peace and quiet to get drunk in," Greasy says. "Where's your horse at, son?"

I couldn't think of no new lie soon enough, so I says, "Carter's Livery Stable, but it ain't ready yet."

"Then you can use mine," Greasy says.

"I didn't agree to race Maggie," the Kid says, sounding worried. "She could beat Taffy without nobody on her at all. It ain't fair. I said *his* horse."

"But look at it logical," Greasy says, like he was explaining ABC's. "You can't race when you're drunk, you'll break your neck. And I can't judge a race fair and square when I'm drunk. So if we have to wait till his horse gets itself shod, the day'll be two-thirds over, and we won't even be drunk yet. Now what's the use of wasting all that time?"

"I'll race him some other day," I says, trying to sound casual.

"He claims he's a rich boy," the Kid says. "Why don't he hire out a horse at the stable?"

"Are you rich, son?" Greasy says.

"To tell the truth, I ain't sure," I says, "but I got mighty good credit."

"That's twicet as good as cash money," Greasy says. "Nobody can borrow it off you. Well, let's go," and he started bowlegged down the boardwalk for a bit, then cut across the street toward the stable, which was around the next corner.

I followed along, heisting my saddle onto my shoulder,

and the Kid commenced untangling his reins and mounting up, and I begun to see there wasn't any earthly way I was going to get out of racing except falling down sick or dying, which wasn't no worse than what a horse could do to me, so I quit worrying.

"Yes, siree, I'll take credit every time," Greasy says over his shoulder. "Packing money's like packing a gun: you're just asking for somebody to take it away from you."

He smelled a little whiffy downwind, but it was a good hard smell, not one of them rancid kind that some cowpokes put out, and it had a sharp layer of whiskey on top of it. "How long does it take to learn to ride?" I says, quiet.

He stopped dead and squinted back at me. "Don't you know how?"

"Well, I could use a little practice," I says.

The Kid hadn't quite caught up yet—he was having trouble getting his pony to go between wagons and cut across the street—and Greasy looked from him to me, then looked me up and down. "I'd say you're on your way to getting a whole crop of lessons, son, which may save you a lot of time in the long run, depending on whether you break your neck or not." He spit past me like he was killing a snake behind me.

The pony come sidestepping cross-legged by us with the Kid making deep quiet noises at her like "Ho, ho, ho," and went around the corner and into the stable yard first, and by the time we got there the Kid had her lashed to a post on a short rein for safekeeping, and all I had to do was figure out some way to keep Lem Carter from making me look like a horse's behind before I could get the job done by myself. I seen him standing on the far side of a string of stalls, leaning back against a stack of hay bales and picking his teeth, and I hurried ahead, toting my saddle, to get a word in before the others could hear me, and I says, "Mr. Carter, you got a nice gentle mare for sale?"

And I seen right away by his face, which was usually white and blank as a clean platter but now had a little smile cracked across it, that the word had got around to him too. He didn't give me no free cigar, but he straightened up to talk to me, just like my old man was along instead of me by my lonesome.

"Matter of fact, I do," he says, keeping his voice down to match mine. "Only twen—only thirty-five dollars, and a better bargain you'll never see in a whole—"

"I'll take her sight unseen," I says. "Could you saddle her up with this?" And I plunked my heap of leather down.

"Why sure, Mr. Holcomb," he says, then hollers, "Amos!" back into the dark.

"What's her name?" I says in a hurry because Greasy and the Kid was coming in after me.

"Missus. Her whole name's Mississippi, only she ain't usually called all of it because folks don't get time," he says just in time for me to turn around and say, "I'll have old Mrs. Sippi saddled up in a minute," but my mouth was all dried out like it gets on a dusty day in the fall when the wind starts pushing the whole prairie through town.

Lem Carter had a kind of stunned look on his face, like somebody's just walked up and handed him first prize, and I could tell it made him uncomfortable to sell a horse so easy. And he was about to keep on selling it to me for a while, so I hurried right on, saying, "Yes, sir, I've had a lot of pleasure out of that horse. I don't know how I managed to do without for so long."

And here I'd been a horse owner for nigh onto three seconds, and I didn't even have to lie no more: the pleasure was real, and I felt just as fond of her as if I'd foaled her with my own hands or growed up with her or been riding her all night for a month and sleeping in the saddle. That lasted about seven more seconds while Greasy nosed around a couple of stalls like he was sniffing out trouble, and then I laid eyes on her, which give me a grand total of ten seconds in Fool's Paradise—a place I have come to believe is a joy to live in but hell to visit.

She was long-barreled and had sort of give up in the middle like a clothesline, though that wasn't too noticeable when the stableboy slung a shredded saddle blanket on her and plunked my spang-new saddle on top of that and filled up the hole. She was a deep chestnut color and had a short chewed-looking tail that wouldn't reach but halfway around her butt when she tried to swat with it, and her ears was a little too tall and her nose a little too fat for comfort. There wasn't nothing for me to do but follow her outside when the boy led her into the yard, trying to keep myself in the way so's the others couldn't get too straight a look at her.

"Yes, sir, you got a real bargain there," Lem says.

"I ain't had a single regret," I says, hoping he'd catch my drift. "She may not look like much, but she's home to me."

"Is that a horse or a moose?" the Kid says.

And, tell the truth, she was kind of taller in the front than behind. But I says, "She can outhop, outskip, and outjump that rabbit of yours, if she's got a mind to."

"Yeah, but can she run?" the Kid says.

Greasy picked up her left forefoot for half a second, looked at it, and let it drop back down like a prospector checking a rock. He says, "Did I hear you say she was getting shod?"

"No, that's next week," I says in a hurry. "Ain't she a beauty?" And I halfway believed it, because I couldn't quite take her all in at oncet and hadn't quite finished swallering the idea I was actually going to have to get up on her. I was still thinking mostly *She's mine,* and I hadn't got around to the next part which is *What do I do with her?*

The Kid was chuckling and looking pleased with himself like he'd just had a load took off his mind, and Greasy says, "Well, we might's well get this over with before I get too dried out to laugh."

"Get what over with?" Lem says.

"Why, these two leather-butted wranglers is going to race," Greasy says.

"Straight west out of town as far as the fork and back," the Kid says, looking happier and happier.

Lem glanced back and forth from the pinto to Mrs. Sippi and says, "Mind holding on till I can locate some of the boys? I wouldn't want them to miss out on no race."

"A race to the finish and may the best man win," Greasy says, "though I expect these two ladies may have something to say about it."

"Now you just wait five minutes," Lem says, his eyes wide open, already shuffling off sideways toward the nearest saloon.

I didn't want to wait and I didn't want to race, and now I'd owned a horse for a minute and a half and didn't want no part of it, and I didn't much want to be doing *any*thing I was doing, yet here I was about to do it. The Kid was untying his pinto and mounting up after hopping around in a circle after it, and I done my best to memorize how he slung his leg up and got his boots shoved into the stirrups, but when I looked back at Mrs. Sippi standing there, I couldn't figure out no connection between her and me. She didn't belong to me, and I didn't belong on her.

"Come on, son," Greasy says. "It ain't no worse than the dentist."

But there was a sight of difference between getting a tooth pulled and having a ton of horseflesh land upside down on you just because you was fool enough to get astraddle of it. Yet I was past recovery now: I had invested my pride in a lie, and there ain't no worse way to make a living. So I started to mount up, already saying, "Ho, ho, ho," to keep Mrs. Sippi calmed down. There ain't but two sides to a horse and two legs on a man, so it stands to reason (unless my arithmetic's wrong as usual) there ain't but four ways to get on a horse, and I since found out three of them's wrong, so actually I done pretty good only being wrong oncet before I hit it right (Greasy got me stopped and recommenced on the left side and left foot in case you want to write that down some place), and there I was, off the ground.

It was the first time I'd been there, and I didn't like it much. The horse was touching the ground instead of me, and she wasn't doing too good a job of it, if you ask me, though she wasn't skittery and flighty and whip-legged like the pinto. The reins was dangling there on the saddle horn and I must of clutched them in a little too tight because her head come rearing back at me and her big long body give a kind of backwards waggle, but then Greasy got aholt of her bit and began leading her out to Main Street where the Kid had already gone zigzagging off.

"You better quit grunting or laughing at her or whatever that is you're doing, boy," Greasy says. "I don't think she reckonizes what kind of animule's on her back yet."

"How do I steer?" I says, whispering.

"Just don't mess with her," Greasy says. "She's got more sense than you, so just let her figure out where to go."

"What if she don't want to win?" I says.

Greasy give me a disgusted look. "You better hope she don't. If she gets any notion like that, you and her's going to part company quick."

We come out into the street with Mrs. Sippi plodding and

plopping and heaving, going slow but not slow enough to suit me, and the Kid was out there on the pinto, fanning back and forth and skidding a little inside a cluster of lunkheads from the saloon. The pinto looked bug-eyed and bothered, and then so did the Kid too because Mrs. Sippi kept going straight on at her (Greasy had let go of the bit and was off behind somewheres) till she come up to the pinto's flank at a right angle and give her a good smell up behind and then at the nose like a dog, and I don't think Mrs. Sippi give much of a durn about the difference between a boy and a girl: she liked the looks of this little rabbity chicken.

Lem was trying to get some bets going, but I couldn't tell whether he got none. I was too busy keeping in the middle of the saddle and trying to recollect everything I'd ever heard about riding which wasn't much.

"On your marks, get set!" one of the lunkheads hollers.

"Shut up!" Greasy yells. "I'm the judge *and* the starter, and I say when."

"Leave me your piece of the Checker, Holcomb," another lunkhead shouts.

"Go!" the first lunkhead yells, and either him or somebody else fired a sixgun into the ground.

The pinto went up in the air off all four feet and was already running before she lit (I had a good chance to watch because Mrs. Sippi didn't do nothing but stand stock still for a few seconds), and her and the Kid went off down a side street in a clump of dust, and I had to look way back over my shoulder to see which way they'd went. But before I could get aimed down Main Street in the right direction, somebody give my horse a big slap on the rump, and she begun a slow lope across the street at an angle to the railing in front of the hardware store where she started smelling up another horse and got herself kicked at. Then she lumbered off along Main Street at a kind of dogtrot, and every time one of her feet hit the ground, that corner of her give a jolt and my nice new rock-hard saddle would come up and jar me right in the firmament (if they can't think of nothing better than leather to make saddles out of, they had ought to quit), the only other trouble being that she was headed east instead of west, switching her head back and forth and taking in the sights like she'd been shut up in the stable all year and had to make up for lost time.

I could hear the lunkheads whooping behind me, but they soon faded out and nobody caught up, so I guess they figured to let me run the race any way I pleased. And in a minute I noticed nobody was paying me much mind along the boardwalk or in wagons, so I must of looked like I was doing things apurpose, which might even mean Greasy and Lem and the lunkheads would think I had pulled out of the race because the Kid was making a fool out of himself, riding off sideways like that, and since one of the main attractions Mrs. Sippi was taking in now was our house (my house?), they might think I'd headed off home disgusted.

The horse didn't pay no attention to reins. I tried one, then the other, then both at oncet, and even tried saying "Ho" again, but all she did was toss her head a little more this way and that. She turned into the lane alongside the house and right past our stable, and I thought of just falling off and calling it a day (she wasn't going fast, just jouncing along steady), but by then I'd had time to get over my first scare and recover some of my natural stubbornness (which couldn't put a patch on hers, but I didn't know that for sure yet), so I just stayed in the saddle (that ain't accurate but you know what I mean) and kept my eyes open and even had a chance to be glad my sombrero was staying on.

We give the hogs and chickens a little workout behind the feed store where Mrs. Sippi took a notion to turn again and head back into town, and I couldn't decide whether to keep my toes in the stirrups and steady myself a little or haul them out and stay ready to sail off if she started doing something I couldn't vote for, so I left one in and one out. She crossed a couple yards and a garden and didn't even get chased by a dog (maybe because they never seen no horse back there before, they didn't know what she was) and squoze between the hotel and Doc Arbuckle's house and come out opposite the jail like she was still looking for something important, and there was the Kid limping back toward Main Street with the back of his shirt tore open and all dusty and no pinto in sight as far as I could see.

He didn't notice me till I was already past, and I says, "Know anybody wants to race?" But I was getting jolted so hard I couldn't say it too good, and I sure couldn't say nothing else either or get turned around to see the look on his face because she took it into her head to swerve left and skin between the millinery shop and a low shed, still going at a steady trot that like to jerk my jaw loose, and I had to hunch and duck to keep from getting hung on a clothesline.

When she come out in the clear again (down a path and through a heap of cans and bottles and between two gateposts which luckily didn't have no gate in them) we was paying the Baptist Church a visit where, if this had been one of them ordinary days that summer, me and Fred would of been making up Bible stories for Pinkus to doze over.

And there on Fred's porch next door, as I went jogging and bouncing by, was Fred and Rev. Haskell (all dressed up like it was Sunday) and my old man's housekeeper in her chocolate-colored crinoline and a bonnet and Mauger in the same dark old clothes but clean-shaved and Shanklin with a folder of papers, and they all gaped at me, and I wouldn't of stopped even if I could of.

And fifty feet further on, here come Pinkus toward Fred's house, trotting and puffing, and he stopped and stared as

Mrs. Sippi went stomping by, with me trying to sit up straight and look like I was heading somewhere deliberate.

But it still wasn't none of *my* choice—Mrs. Sippi only went one way: hers. And when I looked ahead at that thick skull with the big ears sticking out of it and the scraggly mane in between, I couldn't figure out what was inside there or what they were making horse sense out of these days— loco weed, maybe, or just plain old cushion stuffing—though what kept lolloping up and down inside her and making my butt slap the saddle seemed more like some new kind of combine, a hay baler and milk separator and thresher that somebody had stretched horsehide over and turned loose for a joke.

And she picked her next corner sort of unexpected, and while I was getting myself back on straight, she come out onto Main Street again, this time having gained a block in the right direction, so all I had to do was get her to weave through town six or seven more times, and she might hit the fork where me and the Kid was supposed to turn around. And the Kid come limping out down near the lunkheads a few seconds later, and they all commenced talking and pointing this way and that. And Mrs. Sippi hadn't lost interest yet, still switching her head around and drinking everything in, and if you ever seen a dog being whistled at when it didn't know where the whistle was coming from, then you know how she was. It seemed like something was calling her some place and she had to get there, only some idjit had went and hid the place on her.

I just left the reins alone, and burn me if she didn't turn the right way and head out of town, clopping her hooves in the dust and the hard clay and even passing up a couple of slow-moving buckboards. She tried both sides of the street, wandering back and forth whenever something struck her as worth nosing around at, and when we come to the railroad tracks, she looked both ways like as if she'd been trained, and here come the pinto trotting down the right of way by itself, looking in a lather but a little less crazy than usual, and I didn't know what was going to happen now. It could of been anything—the two of them could of crashed or took off up the tracks together or both gone into the depot to set down—but instead they done the last thing I expected: Mrs. Sippi kept right on going toward the fork and the pinto joined up with us, plopping along scatter-legged at the edge of the road which had narrowed down to two wagon widths. When I seen the fork a hundred yards ahead, I didn't know what to do, but it had to be something now because if I stayed on I had a feeling this horse was going to take me over the Divide and across the Snake and straight up and over the Tetons and maybe all the way out into the Pacific till she drownded us both.

And the only thing I could think of was my sombrero, so I took it off when we come to the fork, where one pair of ruts went north and one west, and scrunched forward, shortening up on the reins and half hanging onto her neck with my left arm, and waved it up next to her right eye, between her and the pinto. And she swiveled hard away from it, harder than I wanted but not throwing me, and the pinto shied off the other direction some place. I did it again, and she was scraping through sagebrush and coming around onto the road, heading back for town. I sat up then and put my hat back on and left her alone, feeling as proud as if I'd just busted a bronc, and by the time we got to the railroad tracks again, the pinto had come galloping out of the brush and joined the gang.

Then I seen the Kid running toward us up Main Street, and I got set for trouble, laying as low and steady in the saddle as I could without ruining myself, and I thanked my stars the Kid had enough sense to get off to the side and stand still when we come close or there'd been hell to pay. What he finally done was bad enough: he waited till the pinto was almost even with him, then sprung low before it could jump sideways and caught it by the saddle horn and slung himself up in one steady heave, even though the pony had come jackrabbiting on one leg over into Mrs. Sippi by that time and was commencing to do the polka alongside a little cart.

My horse didn't exactly get out of the way (I don't think she was born to shy at nothing ordinary like another horse), but she turned down the side street nearest at hand like she'd lost interest in racing, with the finish line a block away, and was now looking for new fields to conquer, and when she come within sight of Fred's house and the church again, there was a chunky-looking man in a white suit crossing the road up ahead in a hurry, but he stopped short when he seen me and started hollering, "Holcomb, come here, stop," and things like that which I couldn't do, no matter how much I might want to oblige Mayor Barnshaw, who it was and which wasn't much.

But when I galumphed up even with him, he made a spring at me and got aholt of my arm long enough to pull me way off balance to the right, and he didn't have to do nothing else or keep hanging on nor nothing but just watch while Mrs. Sippi took me six or eight more jounces up the street and I fell off and rolled over a couple times (without losing my sombrero, which come down so far on my forehead I had to pry it off like the lid off a crock).

He was dragging me and brushing at me before I'd even located the difference between up and down and saying, "Come on," and actually I felt kind of relieved and numb in the head and numb in the butt, yet when I seen Mrs. Sippi disappearing in her own dust with my new saddle and realized I was back on my own two feet again, I felt sorry too.

And the Mayor had me up the steps to the front door before I could recollect whether I wanted to run, high heels and all, but he trundled me in ahead of him, not exactly by the scruff of the neck because my bandanna was in the way but sort of, and there was Rev. Haskell in the front parlor with his gray hair all wet down and a look on his face like a man going downhill in a wagon without a horse, and there in front of him was Mauger with his hat off, looking flat-headed and half drunk and mean and worried, and right beside Mauger was the housekeeper with her hand laying in his like a biscuit in a dish, looking flushed and bewildered but kind of happy.

"I now pronounce you man and wife," Rev. Haskell says.

And Pinkus was in the corner looking like a ripe peach, and Fred was peeking around the curtains to the dining room, making some kind of signal at me, and Shanklin was right by the door, white-faced and narrow-eyed, and he grabbed me by the arm as soon as he could reach it.

"What God hath joined together, let no man put asunder," Rev. Haskell says, with a bad taste in his mouth. "You may kiss the bride."

"And then again I may not," Mauger says, gawking around at Shanklin and seeing me. The black look on his face brightened a little, and his upper lip moved and showed a shred of his two front teeth like pieces of bone he had commenced to spit out while eating porkchops.

Between them, the Mayor and Shanklin drug me forward a bit toward Mauger, and the housekeeper turned and shrunk back a ways and looked half scairt, and Shanklin says, "Now shake hands with your new paw, young man."

Mauger held out his hand, but I wouldn't of put nothing in it I expected to see again.

"And kiss your new maw," the Mayor says.

"If he won't do it, why should I?" I says, trying to think, trying very hard, but feeling like I was still thumping up and down on top of Mrs. Sippi.

"That's no way to talk," Mauger says, squeezing his eyes tight till I expected to see blood come out of the corners. "We're all one big happy family here now."

13

————— • —————

The big happy family wasn't feeling any too talkative as far as I could tell. There was some muttering in each other's ears here and there, and Mauger laughed once like he was clearing his throat to spit, but there wasn't no food in sight nor nothing to drink, so I guess the celebration was supposed to be spiritual and refined.

"What happened to my old man?" I says, crowding forward a little and aiming it right at Rev. Haskell. I wasn't scairt of him no more. His face looked like a boiled potato.

"I don't know," he says. "You must try to take your loss with Christian fortitude, boy."

"You've got a *new* paw," Shanklin says. "Try to get it through your head."

"If you don't tell me where my old man is," I says to Rev.

Haskell, "I'm going to foreclose on your church and your house, and you'll have to go to the Checker Casino permanent instead of part-time."

That shocked him to life a little, and he give Shanklin a glance. "He can't do that, can he?" he says.

"Try to take your loss with Christian fortitude," I says.

"Of course he can't," Shanklin says.

"Cooperative, you said," Mayor Barnshaw says, sounding sarcastic. "Amenable, you said."

"The boy's just upset," Shanklin says, squirming a little.

"Just make sure it ain't the applecart," the Mayor says.

The housekeeper was trying to get her hand through the crook of Mauger's elbow, but he kept slipping it away from her, and when she done it oncet too often, he give it a crunch like a walnut, and she yipped.

Shanklin tried to square me around, reaching up to get his hands on my shoulders and scowling kind of earnest and friendly like a schoolteacher who's going to do something for your own good. "I realize the haste of all this may come as a shock to you, young man," he says. "But you have to believe we have your best interests at heart."

"Why do I have to?" I says.

"Because we tell you so!" the Mayor says, raising his voice.

"Now, now, George," Shanklin says. "Young man, there's a liberal fund set aside for your education in the East, and I propose to see that you take advantage of it at the earliest opportunity, even if it means a preparatory school, which it undoubtedly does. You have only to wait a month, and you'll be out of all this. Think of the future, don't dwell on the past."

"He ain't going to get that money," Mauger says. "That's mine."

"Oh, for godsake, Bentley," Shanklin says.

Her face sticking out from behind Fred like a piece of pink candy, Mrs. Haskell says, "Would anyone like coffee?"

"If he wants money so bad," Mauger said, "let him go track down his old man. That's what I done. But he nor no man ain't going to have none of what's mine."

"This is no place for a business discussion," the Mayor says.

Mauger straightened himself up and smoothed some of the wrinkles out of his dark coat. "I'll do anything you say as long as it don't cost nothing," he says, glancing at the housekeeper, then turning his head away with his eyes closed for a second.

"Harvard University is two thousand miles away," Shanklin says like he was making a wish.

"I want to see the papers that make me the son of them two," I says.

"If you insist on knowing the letter of the law, young man, you're going to hear a great many unpleasant things," Shanklin says. "And I don't want to embarrass any of the present company, especially so soon after a wedding ceremony." He made a little dip of the neck at the housekeeper who was keeping as close as possible to Mauger and touching his arm.

"What say we adjourn to the hotel or some place?" the Mayor says.

"That'll be two dollars," Rev. Haskell says.

"For what?" Mauger says. "You ought to paid *me*."

"I think that's a very reasonable fee," Shanklin says.

"If you think it's so blame reasonable," Mauger says, "you pay him."

"Come along, George," Shanklin says, taking the Mayor by the elbow. "I believe the bride knows the way home. She's lived there long enough."

"My fee is two dollars, no matter what kind of blessed

event it may be," Rev. Haskell says. "Without fear or favor, for richer or poorer, in sickness or in health, one price for all."

"Oh, shut up," Pinkus says.

"Since your own interests are involved, Parson, I'd think you might make an exception," the Mayor says.

Rev. Haskell ran his hand alongside his chin where he was sweating. "I can't see it's in my interest to lose two dollars. I've lost enough today already."

"You haven't even started losing yet," Pinkus says. "I'll be foreclosing just as soon as I learn how."

I could see Fred making some new kind of waggles at me from the next room, but I couldn't figure out what he meant. "I hold the church mortgage," I says, "and the parish house too. Ask Mr. Flint."

"I'm afraid there've been some changes since this morning, young man," Shanklin says. "I'm afraid you may find yourself in reduced circumstances."

"He means you're flat broke, kid," Mauger says, letting out a snort. "But don't worry. You're going to come and live at our house where we can look after you proper."

"I want to see the papers," I says.

Raising his voice till it turned thin and sharp and you could saw wood with it, Shanklin says, "I have documents establishing Mrs. Jasper as the common-law wife of Judge Andrew Jackson Holcomb, a document declaring Judge Holcomb legally dead, a document naming me temporary guardian of Andrew Jackson Holcomb, Junior, adoption papers transferring you to the care and keeping of Mr. and Mrs. Bentley Mauger, she being the former Mrs. Holcomb, a marriage certificate for the same, transfers of ownership of all real property, known or unknown, hitherto belonging to Judge Holcomb or to Andrew Jackson Holcomb, Junior—a minor—to Bentley Mauger, Esquire, with the exception of first and second mortgages on the First Baptist Church and parish house of Slope, Wyoming, which go to the Rev. Samuel Pinkus—"

"Don't forget the bicycle," Pinkus says.

"—and one Gent's Utah bicycle," Shanklin says, picking up a black leather folder from the little table next to the dining-room curtains. "Not to mention the finest set of restraining orders I have personally ever laid eyes on, disqualifying and debarring Noah Flint from any exercise of authority over property formerly belonging to Judge Andrew Jackson Holcomb, deceased." And he whipped open the folder with a flourish and showed it emptier than a hog trough at sunrise.

He looked at the inside of it, the outside, the tabletop, the floor, behind the curtains, then begun to turn purple without saying nothing.

"What's the matter?" Mauger says, who must of been the only one in the room needed telling.

After one quick look around at all of us, Shanklin went boiling into the dining room, firing questions and disappearing into the kitchen some place, making more of a racket. Then he come back in a tantrum, dragging Fred behind by the wrist, and set him up straight in front of Rev. Haskell.

"Take a good look at your boy, Parson," Shanklin says. "Because he's on his way to Joliet, Illinois, and the Federal Penitentiary just as soon as I can arrange a cell for him. He burnt my legal papers in the kitchen stove."

But Rev. Haskell wasn't even looking at Fred but at Pinkus, and he says, "How can this here happen when I'm too old to start another church?"

"From now on, it's three dollars per ceremony, cash on the nail," Pinkus says.

"He's going to get ten years for tampering with official government documents," Shanklin says, "and it'll take me the rest of the day to make up a new set. Maybe tomorrow morning."

"I needed something to start the fire," Fred says, but he was looking at the floor and didn't sound like he believed it.

"Him and Holcomb's always conniving something," Mauger says, which might of been true but he was too dumb to prove it.

"Ten years," Shanklin says.

"More like twenty years of hard work," Rev. Haskell says. "Winter and summer. How'm I going to make a living?"

"Go preach in the wilderness, you old fool," Pinkus says. "Or go tell it on the mountain."

I wished there was some way I could help Fred like he helped me, but there was too many of everybody all jammed in the front room now—and Mrs. Haskell wailing like an owl out back some place—so I slipped sideways a bit till there wasn't nobody between me and the door but the Mayor, and I says, "I believe I will bid you gentlemen good afternoon, since I have to go look after my horse."

"Hold it right there, young man," the Mayor says.

"That's right, son, just hold your water," Mauger says.

I got past the Mayor by giving him a little elbow in the watch fob and backed out onto the porch, putting on my sombrero and wishing I could whistle up Mrs. Sippi. "I ain't seen no evidence that gives nobody here the right to tell me where to go or what to do when I get there," I says.

Shanklin bustled after me and come out the door, and at first I thought I was going to have to punch him one in the nose, which could of put me back in jail without a hope, but he went right by and down the steps and halfway out the path to the road.

He turned there and says, "I've got to get back to work,

· 1 4 6 ·

dang it. Don't let the boy get away till I get the papers fixed again."

"We can let the sheriff give him a little tour of the jail-house," the Mayor says.

"No, no," Shanklin says. "The sheriff hasn't quite seen the light yet, and besides, Skin Flint might find him." He kept on going, cutting across the road and disappearing between a shed and a fence.

"I'll take care of him," Mauger says from inside the front room, "just like he was my own son."

So I spun around and jumped down the steps and commenced running across the patches of weeds and clay and got out between the ruts in the road, heading for Main Street and doing the best I could on the high heels which kept catching at the edges of rocks and tripping at me. But I didn't get very far before Mauger had galloped up behind and landed on me, sending us both sprawling forward in the dust. It knocked the wind out of me for a few seconds, or I'd given him a workout, but by the time I could breathe straight, the Mayor was there to hang on too, and the house-keeper, so I decided to bide my time.

From back on the porch, Rev. Haskell says in his Sunday voice, "Thieves and vipers! The sons rise up and smite their fathers, but their tongues shall wither to the root, and the desert shall bleach their bones!"

"Now, now, the neighbors'll hear you, Parson," Pinkus says, standing below him on the steps.

The Mayor come out to the road, shaking his head. "I don't like the looks of any of this," he says. "Just try and keep everything quiet."

"You got them new trousers all dirty," the housekeeper says, half brushing at me and half spanking.

"You may all go to the Devil," Rev. Haskell says.

"Which way's that?" Pinkus says. "I'm a stranger around these parts."

"Well, I haven't seen no papers yet either," Rev. Haskell says, and he went in the house, slammed the door, and shot the bolt.

The Mayor had gone off the same way as Shanklin, looking flustered and wiping his neck and forehead with a white handkerchief, and Mauger—breathing hard through his mouth like a man who ain't accustomed to running fifty feet —give me a shake and says, "No more trouble with you, Junior, or I'll start breaking what little you got left to call your own, which ain't much."

"I'd like to teach that Fred a lesson," Pinkus says, coming out to where we was standing but looking back at the house and frowning.

"You been trying to do that all summer," I says. "Must be kind of discouraging."

Mauger give my arm a squeeze. "There'll come a day, and if it ain't today, it'll be tomorrow. So bide your time, Sammy boy, and you can have Fred and I'll take Junior here. Never can tell: if you peel off some of this sour rind, there might be something inside good enough to eat if we bile it long enough."

"I left my bonnet in the parlor," the housekeeper says.

Looking at Pinkus, Mauger says, "Come on along, Sammy, we got to take this kid home and sit on him till Shanklin's ready."

"Would you mind getting it for me, Bentley?" she says.

He give her a slow tired glance. "Never mind, let's get on home."

"But I can't go down the street wearing this dress without a bonnet," she says. "People'd talk."

"I figured you two might want to be alone, *Bentley*," Pinkus says, smiling nice and sweet and dimply.

"Don't call me that," Mauger says. "And don't talk like a fool."

"I couldn't go without my bonnet, I'd feel nekkid," she says.

"Well, you might's well enjoy it, it's as close as you're going to get," Mauger says, raising his voice a little.

"Don't speak to me that way," she says,

I seen Fred in the parlor window, still making signals at me, but I couldn't any more tell what he meant than I could read Injun smoke.

Pinkus was grinning and enjoying himself, and Mauger says, "Well, we can't stand around here, we'll get picked up for trash. Come on, Sammy."

"You got anything worth drinking at your house?" Pinkus says.

"I don't know," Mauger says. "We got anything to drink?"

"I want my bonnet," the housekeeper says.

Holding his fist an inch from her sharp nose, Mauger says, "I'll give you a bonnet in about a minute, and I'll give you a new face to go with it, which you could sure use. We got anything to drink?"

"Brandy," she says.

Mauger spit off sideways. "Hair tonic. Get a bottle of Red Eye and come on over, Sammy," he says, then paused. "Please."

"All right, all right," Pinkus says, heading off toward Main Street.

And Mauger begun hauling me and the housekeeper the back way to the house, and I went along without no fuss because there was getting to be fewer and fewer people watching me, and sooner or later there might even be none.

And while we was all scuffling along with our mouths shut, I thought maybe this was what it was like to have a real maw and paw and be taking a walk, and it didn't seem like I'd been missing much. I'd never walked nowhere with my old man but what it felt like I had a leash on and couldn't turn or stop unless there was a good reason and maybe not even then. So maybe he was better off not hauling me along when he made a run for it. There's times when you just can't be bothered, and you sure-fire don't expect no useful advice or conversation to start coming from the other end of a leash, nothing to copy down in your Golden Memory Book. But just the same, I wondered if it'd ever be different if I was to run across him again some day after I'd learnt to talk, and then I thought probably not, unless somebody was to learn him how to listen meanwhile which he wasn't too good at.

14

•

All the way home the housekeeper acted like somebody who'd woke up outdoors in the morning without no clothes on and was trying to sneak back to a safe place without meeting the Ladies' Aid Society, and I think she was beginning to wonder whether having a husband amounted to as much as having a bonnet on. But we didn't see nobody to speak of, except when we had to cross a couple lanes, and we got back to the kitchen door without Mauger wasting his breath on idle chatter, which was fine with me because his breath smelled like it had been left for dead.

As soon as she was in her kitchen, the housekeeper quit acting meek and become her old bossy self again, like she was going to test out what this here Mrs. Mauger could do. She put her apron on right over her crinoline, which I had never seen her do before, and she says, "Now you sit down, the both of you."

She meant at the kitchen table, but Mauger didn't know or care and he kept hauling me along, looking this way and that and checking the house over. He seemed to find the study by smelling out the cigars.

"You got to have something to eat," she calls out from the kitchen.

"Drink first, eat later," Mauger says like he was telling her Saturday come before Sunday. "Sammy'll be along." He dug out a stogie from the humidor, bit the end off it, spit it on the carpet, and lit a match by scraping it across the front of the rolltop desk.

I don't know whether the housekeeper could tell a crime like that by sound alone or whether she could feel it happen some place on her skin, same as if he'd tried to scrape a match on the seat of her pants, but she was in the doorway before he'd even got the stogie lit.

"I'll thank you not to abuse the furniture, Mr. Mauger," she says. "We light our matches on the match stand."

Mauger didn't look at her. He pointed at the stool in front of the bookcase and says, "Sit there, Junior," and waited while I done it before he set himself down in my old man's platform rocker and flopped one leg over the arm and begun swinging a dirty boot back and forth. He tipped his hat back and took a long draw on the stogie.

I knew the housekeeper was looking at the little chunk of cigar on her carpet, so I says, "Well, Dad, looks like you bit off more'n you can chew this time."

"What I bite off is either worth chewing, boy, or I spit it out," Mauger says. "I'd say all this here was just an easy supper."

"Don't spit on the carpet," the housekeeper says.

"Why don't you go out in the kitchen and cook up something to keep yourself busy and leave folks alone?" Mauger says.

"Your trousers is too dusty to be sitting in a good chair," she says.

"For instance, why don't you go bake your head?" Mauger says. "Won't nobody eat it, but it would sure quiet things down around here."

I could see the housekeeper thinking that one over, and the frown went deeper between her eyebrows like she didn't care for the tone of voice he was using. "Mr. Mauger, I been meaning to ask where you think we ought to go on our honeymoon," she says. "I hear tell St. Louis is mighty pleasant this time of year if you don't mind the heat."

Mauger took the stogie out of his mouth before it fell out, and he says, "Honeymoon?" like it was some kind of legal term me or Fred had made up to fool him with. "*Honeymoon?* Why, I wouldn't take you on no honeymoon if—if—" He looked around the study like he was trying to find something crazy enough to top her off with, but there wasn't nothing but me and the books. "I'd sooner go on a honeymoon with—" and he had his mouth open to say me, but seemed to change his mind. "No honeymoon," he says. "No time for that stuff."

"I always expected I'd have a honeymoon," she says. "Seems like it wouldn't be a proper wedding without no honeymoon after."

"I'll tell you what," Mauger says. "If you're so set on having one, why don't you go on it by your own self? You probably got some money saved up—" His face changed then like it had just occurred to him to eat a piece of pie. "You got some money saved up, don't you?"

"If I do, that's my business," she says, clamping her mouth shut.

"Husband and wife is on fair shares," Mauger says, sitting

up straight in the chair and flicking ashes on the carpet. "Where do you keep it? In the sugar bowl?" He watched her. "In the cookie jar?" He leaned forward and watched her closer. "In an old sock under your mattress?"

He was getting warm, but *I* wasn't going to tell him. The housekeeper's face got red and patchy-looking. "That's as may be," she says. "I won't have ashes on my carpet. You put that cigar out now, you hear?"

"Why, that ain't your carpet," Mauger says. "That's my carpet. And you don't hardly own the dress you're standing up in no more, if I say so. Is it sewed up in your corset?" He tipped his hat back further and grinned. "I calculate that'd be the safest place."

I could of told him he was doing the wrong thing: the housekeeper was slow to rouse, but when she got up, she didn't come down for days, and till she did, she didn't need no excuse for railing and screeching and carrying on. All a man (or boy) had to do was look at her and she was off again. But Mauger couldn't tell yet what he was building up to.

"I won't have you mention female garments in front of the boy," she says.

Mauger cackled and says, "Maybe it's under a floorboard in your bedroom."

And now he was getting warmer still—in fact, hot—but the housekeeper didn't give him no help. She says, "I hope I'm mistaken, but if these are your true colors, Mr. Mauger, I've been made a fool of."

"You ain't been made nothing you wasn't already," Mauger says.

And sitting there with my back up against all the books I hadn't read yet—and might never read now, if my old man turned out to be dead like he was in Shanklin's burnt-up papers (though it seemed like a lie)—all I could think about was to keep wondering whether the pinto'd made it across the finish line yet or gone busting off sideways some place and whether Mrs. Sippi'd slowed down and turned reasonable.

"You said you'd went and fell in love with me," the housekeeper says, turning her mouth down like a snivel but dry-eyed, which was a bad sign.

"Well, a man's liable to say anything," Mauger says, blowing a big fat lopsided smoke ring.

"You swept me off my feet," she says, which if it was true seemed like turnabout and fair play to me because that's what she done to me many a time when she got the broom going in the kitchen.

"I'm proud to hear it," Mauger says. "Now if I could just shut you up, everything'd be fine."

"Take back your ring!" she says, unscrewing a gold band from her left ring finger.

Mauger stretched out his hand like he'd be pleased to oblige her, but then pulled it back, frowning. "It ain't none of mine. Shanklin found it some place. It ain't nothing but brass."

She threw it backhand into the corner past me, and it bounced around for a second. "Get out of this house!" she says.

"Don't strain your liver bile, woman," Mauger says, looking uneasy for the first time. "We're all in this together."

To keep her spirits up and keep the argument going, I says, "You can't talk to a lady like that in her own house which she's been sweeping and scrubbing all these years."

Mauger switched onto me like he was relieved to have me in mind for a change. "Soon as we get them papers safe and sure, boy," he says, "you're going to find out what it feels like to be a Chinese coolie working on the railroad. I got plans for you." He got up out of the chair and stuck the cigar in his face and come over to my stool and took aholt of the top of my hair like he meant to scalp me, which just goes to show you about taking your hat off indoors: I had mine in my lap where it wasn't doing me no good.

And before I could butt him in the stomach, the housekeeper hit him a good one on the back of the head with the brandy decanter, though his black felt hat broke the blow and kind of scuffed it off his neck. He went down on his knees with his mouth open, still hanging onto my hair, so I didn't even have to get up off the stool—he was there, all convenient, and I landed him one on the jaw. He flopped back on the carpet with his legs twisted under him, and I headed for the front door, it being the nearest way out.

The housekeeper made a clutch at me, but I ducked and shuffled out from under, and she says, "Don't! They'll kill you," lagging behind.

Which was the first I heard of anything on that order. I got the front door open, ready to take care of Pinkus too if he should be coming along with the Red Eye, but he wasn't in sight yet, and I says, "They can't hit what they can't see," and run out and crossed the street, heading for the bank, because I needed some help, and old Flint was the only one I could think of who might know what to do.

And there he was, standing out front of the bank by himself, looking every which way, and when he seen me, he come trotting along like he was afraid of breaking something. When he got as far as Merle's Clothing Store, he slowed down and looked all around behind him and fanned his black satchel at me to slow down, then motioned for me to follow and turned right into the store. By the time I got there, he was already way in the back, talking to Merle, and I heard him say, "Now concentrate, Merle. Can you see me?"

"Yes, sir," Merle says.

"You dang fool, concentrate. Can you see me?"

"No, sir," Merle says.

After the bright daylight, the store seemed gloomy, and when I was almost up to the storage shelves where they was standing, Flint says, "Can you see this young man?"

"I don't know," Merle says, looking hard at Flint. "Can I?"

"No," Flint says.

"That's right," Merle says, relaxing a little and giving a nervous laugh.

"Now go on about your business," Flint says, taking me by the wrist and pulling me around behind a stack of shirts and jeans. "And remember there's nobody back here because you didn't see us."

Merle went away looking worried, and Flint says, "Where in the world have you been, boy?"

"Oh, I've been around," I says.

He put his satchel down on top of a crate and opened the latch. "We don't have much time, so listen to me," he says. "If I had any faith in the limits of man's stupidity, I'd advise you to stay right in your father's house and ride out the storm. But I'm afraid for you—and not just for *you*." He pinched his thin lips forward like a man trying to spend money. "And I don't think I'll be able to protect you much. Or for very long." He reached into his satchel and pulled out a little shammy bag with a draw top and chinked it up and down in his palm. "That's a thousand dollars in gold, and I want a receipt." He laid out a slip of paper in front of me, already wrote out in ink, and handed me a pencil.

And I handed it right back to him to hold while I opened up the bag and made sure they was real twenty-dollar gold pieces, and I had commenced counting them when he yanked the bag shut on me, cussed, and give me the pencil again. So I signed.

And he says, "I'm cashing you out of your education fund which by tomorrow probably won't exist if I know Shanklin. I'd advise you to start broadening yourself with travel immediately, preferably on the sundown train heading east —though the more I hear about this Mauger, the less I like the look of things."

"Mauger's laying on the carpet in my old man's study, trying to remember the laws of assault and battery between husband and wife, which he never did know," I says. "Where's my old man?"

"I don't know," Flint says, "but if I was you, I'd go there too. All he told me was not to bother to write because there wasn't any post office where he was going because every time somebody started to build one, the mosquitoes carried off the logs to pick their teeth with." Flint poked his head around the corner to check the front of the store, then went on almost whispering, "I bought you a train ticket far as Chicago—" he passed me a folded-up ticket, and I stuck it in my pocket "—but after that, you're on your own. Stick that money in the biggest bank you can find, the one with the biggest front door, and they'll help you locate Harvard sooner or later. Get a job. Grow up. Just as soon as you're twenty-one, write me a letter. If you don't hear from me or my wife or my nephew George Flint, that'll be bad news for you, boy, and unless you've found your pa by then, you might as well forget about the gravy train 'cause you missed it."

There was some kind of commotion up front of the store, and when Flint looked, I did too, half expecting to see Mauger there ready to break some bones, but it was a couple of lunkheads from up the street some place, waving their hands at Merle and hollering out some news, and Flint turned back to me and says, "I wish I could do more to help—your pa was always fair and square to me, which wasn't easy for him—but I got a feeling I'm not going to be in the banking business much more'n a day or two, if I know Shanklin, and I've got to protect my own. Any questions?"

His sharp dark little fishface looked at me one eye at a time, switching back and forth and waiting, and I says, "You mean I don't own nothing now but a thousand dollars? I ain't rich?"

"All depends how fast Shanklin is at making out papers," Flint says.

"I went and charged a horse and saddle and some clothes. Do I have to pay now?" I says.

"Those'll be debts owed by Mauger who I understand is your official daddy for the time being."

"Where's all this money coming from?" I says. "All this money that's got everybody chasing theirselves six ways from Sunday?"

"This is a sick town, boy," he says. "Investments are coming in from all over the world. Speculating money: railroads and mines but mostly cattle and land and lately oil, and if you're in a position to help parcel out the results—"

There was more commotion out front, and somebody hollered "Fire!"

"Stay out of sight and try to slip on the train," Flint says. "It's the safest way. They're not worried so much about your pa any more—they figure him as gone for good—but they wouldn't like the idea of you showing up some day with a couple of Philadelphia lawyers in your pocket." He looked me up and down and shook his head. "Maybe you better change to some other clothes while you're here. Help yourself." He motioned at the shelves.

"No thanks, I'll play these," I says.

"Suit yourself, but you look like a—" He fished around for a word, but I guess he couldn't find it. He reached in his satchel and pulled out my old man's thick black belt with the AJH-LLD buckle. "He told me to give you this when you were setting out on your own."

"Well, well," I says, looking it over. It was shiny even in the gloom. "Did he leave town holding up his pants?"

"I believe he had a spare made," Flint says. "Your pa wasn't one to be caught short."

Flint was probably right at that. I'd lived with my old man seventeen years and only caught him short oncet—with the naked dove helping him play rajah. "I'm much obliged to you, Mr. Flint," I says, strapping the belt on, which come around oncet and a half. The buckle looked so big and bright I pulled my shirt out over it.

"Don't let your spirits droop," Flint says. "Keep your dauber up. It isn't so blame hard doing without a father when you come right down to it."

"So I notice," I says. "Everything seems a whole lot livelier."

"You probably had plenty of practice anyway," he says. "Now why don't you just sneak down to one of those shacks near the depot and sit in the shade with your hat over your face. Won't be more than an hour if the train's on time." He turned thoughtful and quieter, rubbing his long face with a skinny, shaky hand. "Maybe they'll calm down when they quit worrying about you. Maybe they won't have to shoot anybody. They'll see they can do it all on paper."

"Shoot who, for instance?" I says.

"Go on, get out of here," Flint says, heisting up the bar on the back door and pushing it open a slit. "Use your brains, and keep that money some place where it won't fall out every time the train runs over an Injun."

I was going to thank him again, but he shoved me out and shut the door on me, so there wasn't nothing to do but stow the moneybag in my hip pocket and the ticket in my shirt and start for the depot. But when I come out of the back lane behind the bank, I could see the people straggling out of the Checker Casino and heading off toward big clouds of smoke somewhere behind the courthouse, and when I ducked across and hurried along to the next cross street and give it a good look, I seen it was the Baptist Church.

I joined up with a bunch of lunkheads following the leaky water wagon down the street to Fred's house, which was going up in smoke and flame too and saving Shanklin the trouble of making out one set of papers that afternoon. Some of the boys had got out the buckets and even filled up a few from the spigot back of the wagon, but then there wasn't much more to do than stand there and watch. They couldn't get close enough to do more'n water the bushes halfway up the path. It was going to be a short fire but a hot one, and I couldn't help thinking Rev. Haskell had got part of what he kept promising everybody else, only it wasn't quite as eternal as he'd allowed it would be. It was only going to last about ten minutes, if that, and I remember thinking maybe Baptists ain't got a whole lot to burn, but what they got burns good and proper, and then the tin-can roof fell in, and Fred's house sort of shifted sideways and tipped over into it, and both me and Pinkus was out of one job, each having been a landlord for only a couple hours apiece.

Old Flint had told me to use my brains, but you can't do something like that apurpose. It has to happen in its own sweet time, so it wasn't till both places was dang near flat on the ground, looking like pits of coals for a barbecue, that I figured out Rev. Haskell had probably done it, and I begun to look around and hope hard he hadn't decided to cook Fred too just to prove something. I kept out of the crowd now, a couple houses away, ready to run if somebody showed any signs of chasing me, and I seen Pinkus before he seen me. He was up as close as he could get without turning

his potbelly into pork cracklings, and he was cussing the fire
—or I judged he was. He had both fists clenched at it and
was talking steady, bobbing his fat head now and then for
emphasis when he hit a good one, and I backed off further
down the street.

I wanted to help Fred, but there wasn't no way to do it
without finding him, and I didn't know where to look. I cut
across Main Street again about a block from the Checker,
near what was supposed to be the finish line in the race be-
tween me and the Kid, but there wasn't no sign of him or
Greasy or the pinto or Mrs. Sippi except for a string of horse
apples which could of been anybody's. So I used my brains
and headed for the depot, traveling light, with nothing but
what I stood up in, no horse, no bicycle, no home, no old
man, and nothing to worry about except the future.

15

———— • ————

But the future wasn't as far off as I figured it to be, and there was so much of it and it come at me so thick and regular I didn't have much time for thinking, let alone worrying. No, that ain't quite true. There was *one* thought—if a question counts as a thought—that kept coming up. It wasn't the first time I'd had it, but now it was coming about every hour like clock chimes, and it amounted to *What am I now?* I felt like I was changing, and every now and then I'd catch myself up short and ask it. Sometimes I could squeeze out half an answer, but mostly I just plain stuck myself like I was my own teacher asking for the principal parts of some blamed word or other or the principal rivers of the world.

Everything I did now, I could see myself doing it right before my eyes, which was a relief sometimes because it wasn't just me hitting Mauger in the face, for instance, but this young cowboy wearing a bandanna and boots. I don't know what it meant, but something had broke loose inside me and was on its own.

So when I set down in the shade and leaned back on one of the sheds near the depot where I could keep an eye on the tracks and along Main Street by shifting my eyes a little under my sombrero, I seen myself doing it, and up come the old What am I now? And I got a brand-new answer which was you're a young cowpoke that started the day too early, and now you're waiting it out to see if it looks any better in the dark, because if it don't, you're going to have to head back to the Broken B or the Lazy Z or some place on foot, hungry, since you lost a month's pay in the Checker and got hornswoggled out of your horse by a couple of slickers, and you don't want to do nothing now but doze away the daylight.

And I got to feeling so much like that, I thought Mauger or Pinkus or Shanklin or the Mayor could walk right by me and not give me a second look. But then Fred had to go and spoil it by plopping down next to me, winded and sweating and kind of wild-looking, and saying, "Jackson, I don't know what to do."

"Well, you could join up with some other church that ain't been burnt down yet," I says.

"My old man's gone loco," he says. "He's gone to live at the Checker Casino, and my ma's been carted off by a bunch of church ladies, and I didn't want to go with neither one of them. I seen you watching the fire." He fanned himself with his cap, and I could tell he was looking over my cowpuncher's outfit.

"It was a right nice fire while it lasted," I says. "Maybe I could hire your old man to do it to mine."

Fred looked surprised. "How'd you know he done it?"

"He had it in him," I says, not really knowing what I meant. "I got a train ticket to Chicago."

"I was thinking about the train too, but I ain't got any money," Fred says. "Suppose I could sneak on?"

"I'll see what I can fix up for you," I says, because I still hadn't got over feeling like a rich boy. "First off, you're going to need some different clothes. You want to look growed up, don't you?"

"Sure," he says, his eyes wide. "My Sunday suit burnt up."

"Well, come on then," I says, getting up. "The train won't be in for an hour. We got to sneak back to Merle's." I figured if my credit was still good I might's well chalk up some more to Mauger.

We done it by all the back ways, though most of the loafers and lunkheads was still up watching the fire go out and telling each other where they was standing when the roof fell in, and Merle let Fred have some jeans and a couple shirts and a jacket, marking it up to my account and only looking a little worried until I mentioned Skin Flint's name a couple times to remind him how me and the bank was close enough to be kin. So there was Fred's brown shiny woostered everyday suit laying on the floor with the sleeves about five inches too short and the pants legs leaving off about five inches too high and the elbows patched and the seat needing a patch it was never going to get, and Fred never even looked at it again. Merle didn't have no sombreros, just a couple styles of straw Stetsons, but Fred didn't know no better, and he found one that fit and crunched it on, and the first thing you know, he looked pretty near as old as me.

This time Merle made me sign a sheet of paper, so I gritted my teeth and wrote "Andrew Jackson Holcomb Junior Mauger" just to make sure the money got blamed onto the right party, and we was out the door before Merle could do more than commence wondering.

I think Fred probably felt sort of drunk, like I did, being in a mess of trouble yet not really minding so much because it was a *new kind* of trouble. He'd walked about ten feet toward the bank in his new clothes, when he stopped in the shadow of a store front, with the deep-red sunshine just beginning to peel up off the street and light out for the West, and he looked around at the town and me and down at himself, and he says, "Do you feel funny?"

And I says, "Yes," knowing exactly what he meant.

"I keep thinking there's something I'm supposed to do," he says, "but every time I start to do it, I won't."

"I won't neither," I says.

Fred looked all around again. "It feels like sinning."

"That's right," I says.

"But whatever it is, at least it's mine," he says. "And the trouble feels like somebody else's. It ain't none of mine."

"You and me both," I says, feeling proud of Fred who was making up for lost time as fast as I was. And right about then I remembered I was supposed to be hiding out and not getting caught by Shanklin or the sheriff, and the reason I remembered was old Skin Flint stuck his head out the front door of the bank which had the CLOSED shade pulled down it again, and he says, "Dang it, boy, are you out of your mind?"

"No, sir," I says, jumping near to the corner.

"The train's due in," he says in a shouting whisper. "You catch it or there'll be hell to pay."

"Yes, sir," I says, ducking off to the right in a hurry with Fred trailing me past the side of the Checker on the other side of the street and aiming for the back lanes. "Which floor's your old man going to live on?" I says.

"I don't know." Fred kept looking back at the privy and the rear door of the casino like he might have a crack at finding out first-hand.

"Come on, now," I says, leading the way a little faster. "Least you know where he is." Which I meant to say was more'n I knew about mine.

And we'd started scooting along again when we heard two shots from inside the Checker some place—or they sounded like it—and then another one by itself while we was stopped to listen. They didn't have that outdoor sound, didn't raise the right kind of flapping echo but was muffled a little.

Fred was scowling and looking scairt at the same time, so I says, "That's just Lulu teaching somebody how to dance," but I ain't sure that's what I believed.

"My old man don't know one end of a gun from the other," Fred says.

"It don't take long to learn," I says. "I expect that was Simon learning himself how to draw."

Then there was two more shots from further away off toward the bank but still with that indoor sound, and I says, "The Checker and the bank is going to shoot it out to see who runs the town."

"You think I ought to go look?" Fred says.

"You just said it wasn't no trouble of yours," I says, trying to lead the way again, shuffling between the tin cans. "I don't know of nobody else in town who can buy you a ticket to Chicago and points east such as Harvard Law School, and I ain't going to be around much longer to do it."

Fred come along then, and pretty soon he was going as fast as me, and we come out of the tangle of shacks and lean-tos and scraggle-sided shanties with the dogs barking at us, and there was the depot with what looked like the same people slumping around on the platform and no train in yet. I stopped there, about fifty yards off, and pulled my sombrero down tighter and leaned up against a corner post and begun waiting again.

"Ain't you going to buy me that ticket?" Fred says, looking from me to the depot.

"I'll buy it on board," I says. "It's safer."

But the more I talked about it and the closer it come to being real, the less I wanted it, and the mere mention of law school had started making me sick—though it didn't seem to bother Fred none—and while I was standing, feeling worse and getting younger and dumber and sadder by the minute, along come my Fate and my Destiny, which didn't look like nothing of the kind.

It was the Kid on the pinto and Greasy on a muscly short-barreled hard-looking bay horse, leading Mrs. Sippi by the reins. She still had my new saddle on her and was actually following somebody and doing what they wanted, which was a big surprise to me.

When he seen me and Fred, Greasy veered over our way and reined up, though the pinto and Mrs. Sippi didn't stop scuffling and bumping and rearing around for a few seconds. Handing me the reins, Greasy says, "Here, take this dang thing, will you? We been looking all over town for you."

I took aholt, expecting to get pulled up by the roots, but Mrs. Sippi just stood there looking around like she'd come to wait for the train too. "I'm much obliged to you," I says. "I had to get off her and go to a wedding, otherwise I'd of took care of her myself. I guess we'll have to finish that race some other time."

The Kid put back his head and laughed, and the pinto jigged backwards, almost going out from under him. Steadying her finally, he says, "I come across that finish line first, and just because you wasn't there to see it, don't cut no ice with me. I got witnesses, ask Greasy here."

Greasy shook his head and nodded both, and I says, "Well, when I met up with your horse out there at the turn and you wasn't on it or under it or chasing it, I figured you'd quit."

The Kid opened his mouth to start arguing again, but Greasy says, "You both lost if you ask me, so shut up about it." He looked a little wobbly in the saddle, but he didn't sound drunk. "I'm the judge, and I call it a draw—Junior won the first half and the Kid the second."

"It don't mean nothing to win the first half of a race," the Kid says. "All that counts is the finish."

"Dry up, Kid," Greasy says, and he smacked his lips like he just dried up himself. He tried to spit but nothing come out. "It's Friday night, and we ain't in jail, and we had a whole week off work."

"Where you headed?" I says, afraid they might go away because Greasy was switching his head all around like Mrs. Sippi.

He stopped then and looked down at me, leaning one elbow across his saddle and propping his other hand on his hip, and he says, "Son, it don't seem possible, but I'm going back to work. I let the Kid here talk me into it. We got two days of riding if we're going to be there before Monday. We got nothing to drink and no place to sleep and no money, so we was riding off from the—"

"So's you wouldn't sell your horse like you done my carbine," the Kid says.

"—from the temptations of the city to bed down under the stars, sober and useless and boneheaded like all cowboys when they got to have that dollar a day," Greasy says, lifting one hand and raising his voice.

And I still don't know why I done it, but when I heard him talk—not so much the words or the idea of working and sleeping outdoors—but just the way he was saying it, deep and rough yet kind of singing, well, I started getting my own ideas, and I thought of that long train ride into no place and maybe a big school at the end of it, so I says, "How long does it take to learn to be a cowboy, Mr. Brown?"

"It ain't a matter of learning much," Greasy says. "It's more like forgetting what you think you know already."

The Kid was laughing again. "Mr. Brown!" he says, mocking.

"What's wrong with that?" Greasy says. "That's respect for my years and the gray in my beard, and you could use a little of it yourself."

"What do you get for the baccy juice in your beard?" the Kid says.

"You reckon you could teach me and my friend to be cowboys?" I says, because I'd commenced thinking of another kind of college altogether.

"I reckon I could if I felt like it," Greasy says. "I could if anybody could. But I don't happen to have no cattle on me to teach you with." He pulled his old crushed hat around this way and that like he was trying to find the grooves in his head and blinked off at the last shreds of sunlight coming across the railroad tracks. "You better go on and think about regular schooling, boy. You got to be born dumb and pore and stubborn and thirsty if you want to be a cowboy or else you can't stick it out."

"Do I want to be a cowboy?" Fred says, looking puzzled.

"Well, you don't want to be no preacher's son," I says. "And you don't want to live with a bunch of Baptist ladies, do you?"

"I thought I wanted to go to law school," he says.

"All right," I says. "You can have my ticket as far as Chicago, and good luck to you. All you got to do is walk another thousand miles after that, then find out where they hand out the shingles to Wyoming boys who ain't learnt their Latin yet." I turned to Greasy again. "I'm dumb and stubborn and pretty thirsty, and I'm going to be pore later on, but right now I'll pay you a dollar a day to teach me and him all there is about cowboying."

The Kid looked mad and nervous, and he says, "Come on, Greasy, it's going to be dark before long."

But Greasy kept staring at me and Fred and looking thoughtful and giving his horse little touches on the neck to hold her still. "How long was you figuring on studying at this Cow College of mine?" he says.

"Till we quit or you call us cowboys, one," I says.

"We ain't got time to fool around," the Kid says. "Come on, Greasy, somebody else'll have the sand patch before we get there."

"A dollar a day?" Greasy says, still looking at me and Fred.

"Paid day by day if you want it," I says.

"Where's his horse?" Greasy says, nodding at Fred.

"I ain't even made up my mind yet," Fred says in a high voice.

"And where's your blanket rolls, both of you?" Greasy says.

Off in the distance I heard the thin wailing toot of the train, and I says, "I'll buy whatever we need, but we got to get on out of here before long."

There was some more of what sounded like gunshots back toward the middle of town, and Greasy jerked his head that way for a second to listen. "They're starting the fun early," he says, kind of wistful.

"Don't be a dang fool," the Kid says. "Rafferty is going to fire you sure if you're late again."

"Who says I'm going to be late?" Greasy says, then to Fred: "What say, boy? You figure to learn cowpunching on foot?"

"Well, if I had a horse, I'd try," Fred says, timid and hesitating. "I can always go to school next year."

Greasy started glancing all around again, and finally he settled on the depot where some people had showed up to catch the train or meet it and where the biscuit-heads and loungers just come over to see something happen besides horseflies in front of their face, and Greasy says, "Gimme that ticket. No use letting it go to waste."

So I handed it over, and Greasy trotted his horse down the slope to the edge of the platform next to a couple raggedy-looking horses tied to the rail there and got off and climbed up onto the warped planks and started nudging a passed-out cowboy with his foot. The cowboy had his hat over his face and his legs sprawled crooked and his shirt half-open, and Greasy lifted up the hat and said something to him, then turned and said something to a cowpoke setting with his back propped against the station, who jerked his thumb at one of the horses.

The train was puffing into sight now, coming out of the purply murk where the sun had already sank, and the Kid says, "How about if I teach you a couple of things too?"

"I got no objection," I says. "But I guess I'd better leave that up to Mr. Brown. Me and Fred take our tutoring serious, don't we, Fred?"

"Sometimes," Fred says, sounding doomed.

"You going to pay *me* a dollar a day?" the Kid says.

"Maybe, if you earn it," I says.

The engine, with a chimbley like a stove-pipe hat somebody sat on, come chugging into town, pulling three cars behind, and squeaked its brakes all the way past the depot and across the road in front of us, but we could still see Greasy through the windows, and now he was dragging the cowpoke upright and stuffing the ticket in his pocket and loading him forward onto one of the cars like a sack of oats.

"You ain't doing Greasy no favor by getting him off on some cork-headed idea like this," the Kid says. "If he loses his job at the ranch, won't nobody hire him no more. He's already worked every other place for two hundred miles around, and he's getting too old to cut it. He's too proud to cook or horse-wrangle, and he can't hold his liquor too good no more, and you could finish him off just fooling around."

"We won't get in the way," I says, hoping it was true. "You just get him where he has to be, and we'll ride along." I shortened up on Mrs. Sippi's reins a little, remembering what it was like to be on her. She didn't stir, and for the first time I give her a good look in the eye, and she was gazing right at me—or through me, I don't know—and my heart come partways up my throat for a little exercise.

"But I don't know how to ride," Fred says.

"It's easy," I says. "You just hang on till you fall off, then you get back on as soon as you can catch the horse. That's the way me and the Kid do it."

The train was puffing again but standing still, and Greasy come around the front end on his horse, leading a scraggly dusty bony long-nosed rump-sprung gelding with two bed-rolls on it and sassing back at the engineer who leaned out of his cab to handle his part of the conversation.

When he come up to us, Greasy says, "I swapped him the ticket for the horse and bedroll, and his buddies was so glad to see him go, they threw in the extra roll. Give them something to talk about." He handed the reins to Fred and took a look around at the sky. "Name's Buster. Well, we might's well get going, unless you want to get your first lesson navigating by moonshine." He glanced at the Kid. "I mean moonlight."

The Kid shook his head, looking disgusted, and didn't say nothing, and Fred says, "How do I get up?"

Greasy give a little jerk like he'd just been half asleep, and he leaned way sideways to stare at Fred. "Which way do you figure on facing?" he says.

"Same way he is," Fred says.

"That's a good idea," Greasy says. "In that case, you can

get him by the tail and come up hand over hand, or you can stick your left foot into that stirrup on the left flank and sling your right leg up. Unless you want to ride rear-guard duty facing the other way to make sure nobody's chasing us."

"I don't mind," Fred says.

The Kid laughed, and Greasy says, "No, better face front-ways till one of us shoots somebody or does something ornery enough to get possied."

Fred mounted up like he was climbing a ladder and got his foot caught in one of the bedrolls and lost aholt of the reins, and Greasy had to sidle over and get him settled. The engine give a hoot, and the Kid's pinto put her ears back and ducked her head at it like a bull.

Keeping a tight rein, the Kid says, "How do you know he's got any dollar a day? He talks big, but when it comes to pay up, it'll be Nellie bar the door."

I didn't want to show nobody my shammy bag, so I says, "Looks to me like two greenhorns doing what we're doing has to trust you two more'n a dollar-a-day's worth."

The engine give two more toots and went chuffing and chugging and sparking down the track, slow as a wagon at first but picking up steam, and a couple of the lunkheads on the platform was hoorawing at the cowpoke who was going to wake up in Kansas some place, and Greasy says, "If he don't sleep too long, he can trade in half the ticket for a ride back," and that felt like a comfortable way to look at it.

"Well, it don't seem too hard yet," Fred says, setting there on Buster who hadn't even moved a tail muscle.

Swiveling and hushing and hanging on, the Kid kept the pinto from flying off the handle over the engine noise, and when I seen the coast was clear and nothing wild or loud or sudden was happening, I swung up on Mrs. Sippi, clung on and waited, but she held almost still, just glancing around at me like she wanted to see who she was saddled with now.

"Well, come on," Greasy says. "I sure get some funny ideas when I'm sober, which is the sad story of my life. If I'd been born rich, I could of kept enough whiskey in me to make my brains work all the time. I could of been one of the lords of the land." He switched his reins about a quarter of an inch, and his horse give a half turn and started along the road.

"Instead of just one more dang old fool," the Kid says, his pinto skipping along after.

"Watch your tongue, Kid," Greasy says. "Cowboy College is in session now, and you got to give the perfesser his due respect."

I found I didn't have the nerve to touch Mrs. Sippi with my heels or even to flick the reins, but before I could disgrace myself, she started on her own, with her nose almost up the pinto.

Fred's horse begun slumping along too, after starting and stopping a couple of times, and we was underway in the half darkness and across the tracks toward the fork, and when some more muffled shots come from back of us in the middle of town, I didn't give a durn who was aiming at who. And this time when that voice asked me, *What am I now?* I had an answer for a change. "I'm a cowboy," I says.

"What's that?" the Kid says.

"Nothing," I says, trying to get used to the buck and weave of the saddle.

16

We hadn't gone bumping along more'n a couple hundred yards past the fork, heading west, when Greasy turned his horse left off the road and commenced scraping between big clumps of brush that come halfway up his shins, and he was almost out of sight in the shadows in about two seconds. The Kid followed him in, and I did too (I mean I didn't do nothing to prevent Mrs. Sippi using her own horse sense on the subject) and, judging by the noise behind, I reckoned Fred's horse wanted company. We all went down into a hollow with sides steep enough to make me hope Mrs. Sippi didn't get some kind of running start I couldn't stop, but she went down deliberate, like an old lady going downstairs, and I didn't have nothing to do but keep the sorest parts of my rear end from hitting the saddle too many times in a row. I tried to make them take turns.

Fred beat me into camp (which it turned out to be) by falling off his horse and rolling past me into a yellowy-white clump I found out later was sand, but his horse come along by himself, and nothing got busted or lost, and by the time I'd clumb down, shaking, from the saddle, Fred was up and brushing himself off.

"I only fell off oncet," he says. "That's pretty good, ain't it?"

It seemed like we'd been riding for hours, but I knew it was only about ten minutes, and I couldn't figure out why we was settling down so close to town. I'd of been glad to put a couple more miles between me and Mauger, no matter how my rear end felt, but I could see Greasy tethering his horse to a bush and hobbling it and the Kid unwinding his bedroll on the sand, so I done the same and Fred copied me, and pretty soon we'd all finished unsaddling the horses and propping our saddles at the heads of the bedrolls like backlogs for a fire, and Greasy was laying down inside his blankets, grunting and sighing while he wiggled to shape the sand under him.

"Should I start a fire?" I says. "I know how to do it."

"What for?" Greasy says.

"Well, I don't know," I says, watching the Kid lay down and wiggle inside his bedroll too. "I thought camps had to have a fire." It was getting so dark now I couldn't see their faces no more.

"Well, we ain't got nothing worth cooking," Greasy says, "but if you feel like making one to look at, why, go ahead."

I hadn't thought about food since my big breakfast, but I begun to feel empty now. Yet when I heard the Kid snickering, I knew I couldn't mention it and give him the satisfaction. "I thought it was to scare off critters or something," I says.

"We ain't got anything they want," Greasy says. "But if you want to make yourself useful, you and what's-his-name there can go over to the water tank and fetch the horses a drink."

I'd thought it was a dim gray boulder on the far side of the sand, but now I seen it was a water tank and we was back beside the railroad tracks. "What'll I fetch it in?" I says.

"You got a hat on, ain't you?" Greasy says.

So me and Fred groped our way to the tank and looked it over best we could, and there wasn't nothing for it but one of us had to get on the other's shoulders to pull down the hinged spout, and I knew sure as fire somebody was going to get wet, and it turned out to be both of us. I went up on Fred, caught the spout, and brung it down, but he let go of me too fast, and it was gushing and playing all over before Fred could steady it and let me fill up my hat, and then with my hat full, I didn't have no way to steady the spout for Fred, so he had to try holding his with one hand, and it took him a couple of tries and a couple of dousings to do it. Then we come stumbling back with a hat and a half full of water, spilling some more, and them horses didn't get much more'n a smell of it, though Mrs. Sippi seemed to like Fred's hat fine and took a chunk out of the crown, since we'd forgot it was straw.

When we'd finished our first chore as cowboys, we stood around for a while, fanning our arms back and forth to dry off, and I says, "Where'd this here sand come from?"

Sounding half asleep already, Greasy says, "Some idjit tried to start a glass factory, but they went and dumped his sand off at the wrong spring, and when he finished suing the railroad, he didn't have enough money left to fetch the sand to the right place or even probbly to keep a fire going, so let that be a lesson to you to keep out of your old man's courtroom. Now shut up and go to sleep, both of you, unless you want to do night watch."

"How do you do that?" Fred says.

The Kid started snickering again under his blanket, and Greasy says, "Well, you just keep an eye on it, son. You watch it. And if it starts doing anything it hadn't ought to, then you shoot it."

"I got nothing to shoot it with," Fred says.

"Then holler at it," Greasy says. "And we'll wake up and do the shooting."

I fanned myself some more and waved my hat back and forth, and Fred seemed to think that over. "How do I know what it is if I can't see it?" he says. "I mean it might be something friendly like a stray horse."

"What you got a nose for?" Greasy says.

"I don't know," Fred says.

"You got to be able to smell trouble if you're going to be the night watch," Greasy says. "Trust your instinks. If you think it's trouble, most likely it is. Shoot first and ask questions later."

"I thought you didn't pack no gun," I says.

"Who's the perfesser around here anyways?" Greasy says, thrashing around a little in the dark. "If you're going to start all this, I'll have to charge a dollar a night too."

"Maybe Jackson better be the night watch," Fred says.

"Oh, shut up and go to sleep," Greasy says, and the Kid snickered some more.

Fred was quiet for a while, and then he says, "What's the night watch do when it comes daytime?"

"Why, he just stands back and lets her come," Greasy says.

"I mean when's he get to sleep?"

Raising his voice and making the horses scuffle and shift a little, Greasy says, "The best kind of night watch is half asleep night and day so it adds up to the same thing."

Fred kept quiet again and did some more fanning, and I could hear the air whooshing through his hat where it was tore open. Then he says, "I don't think I'd be any good at it."

"All right then," Greasy says. "You go on to sleep, and *I'll* be the night watch."

"That's fine," Fred says, sounding relieved. "Maybe I'll get the hang of it."

Greasy groaned and thrashed around some more, and because I felt about half dried, I knelt down and tried to peel open the right layer of my bedroll, which didn't smell too bad considering it'd been a hot summer, and I could see the faint outline of Fred next to me, doing the same thing, but before we'd pulled off our boots to get in, Greasy was snoring.

Fred quit moving and seemed to listen awhile, and then he whispers, "I don't think he's watching too close."

In a low voice, the Kid says, "Shut up, greenhorns."

I'd used the word myself, so I couldn't quarrel with it now. I kept quiet and tried to half sit against the saddle and pretended to be happy, which I didn't know whether I was or not. Being a cowboy seemed mighty uncomfortable.

"Are you scairt?" Fred says, whispering.

"No," I says, not exactly lying.

"Then I ain't either," Fred says, squirming and sliding his knees around inside his bedroll, trying to make a dent in the sand.

After that, things seemed to settle down, except me. I laid my head back on that new leather with the smell of it stronger than fresh straw in a mattress and tried to keep my eyes closed, but every time I shut them, something seemed to crack them open again, and I'd be staring at the dim clouds coming apart overhead and beginning to let the stars out and all the rest of the smears and streaks and daubs up in the sky that neither Mauger nor Pinkus could tutor us anything about. I kept looking, and I didn't know the name of nothing. The moon hadn't come up yet, if it was coming up at all, so I couldn't count that. And it made me feel bad.

And the quieter it got, the noisier it got, which was the first lesson I learnt on the prairie: just as soon as the grunts and whickers and scratchings and scrapings—and all the rest of the small commotions people and horses make without half knowing it—just as soon as they simmer down, then you start getting acquainted with what you don't know. Greasy left off snoring all of a sudden, and in the deep quiet that come after, I begun to hear all kind of things I never heard before. It was the same as staring at a piece of night sky that looks empty, and pretty soon you can see more and more stars in it. I heard the brush crackling nearby and expected sure enough to have some shaggy critter with a mouth full of teeth come lurching through to jump us or the horses, but minute after minute, nothing happened.

I heard hoots and whistles and squawks and long-drawn-out wails and howls, some from so far away they seemed like they must of come from town or even from the mountains which you can't hardly see on a clear day. Fred was asleep before I could ask him whether he was asleep, and Greasy and the Kid didn't stir, so for a while at least I turned out to be the night watch. I was spending the first night of my life outside of a bed, and there was a stubborn glum-faced slit-eyed part of me that couldn't see no particular advantage in it and was considering getting up and hiking back along the railroad tracks to town and setting up shop in the hotel or maybe in the Checker Casino and forgetting this foolery. Yet there was another part of me (and it was stronger) that felt like it was right where it belonged, stiff neck, sore behind, and all, and was ready to start singing "Buffalo Gal" and growing a beard and carrying its belongings in my pockets and smelling like cattle. I already smelled like Mrs. Sippi, so I was getting there, and then sleep snuck up on me after what seemed like a long long day and jumped me like an Injun and laid me out cold, and there wasn't nobody left to watch.

17

———— • ————

I woke up bent permanent like a horseshoe, and for a while
it seemed like my big chore of the day would be to get stood
up proper without hunching like old Archer that got sat on
by a steer when he wasn't looking and been walking around
ever since like he was prospecting for gold. But I got
straightened out in a couple minutes, and it was cold dawn
with a low mist tumbling slow along the tracks like old
steam, and Greasy was lifting a coffeepot off two small flat
stones that had a little fire bustling between, using his ban-
danna on the handle and filling the Kid's cup first, then his
own, and dunking a brown hard-looking chunk of something
in it, then gnawing and sipping and dunking, and the Kid
doing the same.

"Morning, Junior," Greasy says when he seen me looking. "I see you survived the raid all right. That's good."

Fred come rearing up out of sleep next to me, staring around with his hat on crooked and his eyes half open, and I says, "What raid?"

"Just in time to get your first lesson of the day," Greasy says. "It's what cowboys do instead of praying: them that has cups gets coffee first, and them that don't have cups has to wait and learn how to squeeze it out of the grounds. There's a trick to it."

"What raid?" I says. "I didn't hear no raid."

"And the second lesson is corndodgers," Greasy says. "There's two kind of men in this world: them that thinks they're edible and them that thinks they ain't nothing but young rocks that need exercise."

"The second kind get mighty hungry the second day," the Kid says, his jaw working.

I stood up slow and kicked my legs around a little and tried to bend my belly forward, using both hands on my hips, then had to crouch to pick up my sombrero because my spine felt like a stack of broken glass.

"Is it morning?" Fred says kind of blurry.

"Well, if it ain't," Greasy says, "God has went and made an awful mistake back East."

"What raid?" I says. ·

"Didn't you hear it?" the Kid says with his mouth full.

"I was scairt to move, let alone give a signal," Greasy says. "So I figured you two was better off asleep because you'd keep quiet. What do you reckon it was, Kid? Shoshones?"

"I don't know. Some kind of war party," the Kid says.

"They never did get all the way around us, or I'd of woke you sure," Greasy says. "Heading for town to steal horses, maybe, and ours wasn't worth the commotion."

"How do you know it wasn't white men?" I says. "There

ain't enough Injuns within a hundred miles to get up a poker game."

Greasy finished his coffee and wiped his beard with the back of his buckskin sleeve and scowled at me. "Do you have to look out the window to tell whether it's a brass band or a herd of sheep going down the street? I know what I hear, and many's the white man been given a Dakota haircut by Injuns that was supposed to be a hundred miles away."

"When do we eat?" Fred says.

"Why, what do I look like I'm doing?" Greasy says, pouring himself another cup of coffee and reaching down to pull another corndodger out of his saddlebag.

"I mean us," Fred says, looking at me and hesitating. "Or me."

"Well, I'll have to think it over," Greasy says. "I didn't know I was throwing in board as well as lodging at my college. I may have to reconsider my fee."

"I ain't about to pull cook duty for no greenhorns," the Kid says.

I begun to get the idea, so I says, "Excuse me," and headed off in the bushes a minute, and while I was there I got out my shammy bag and dipped in for my first twenty-dollar gold piece and come back with it and held it out over the coffeepot and says, "Let's see how far this here'll go for room *and* board."

The Kid's eyes sprang open, and Greasy stood up and took it and give it a little bite, sticking it way back in his jaw where he could find two teeth that come together, and he had his saddle up on his shoulder and his horse blanketed and cinched and was up on it before the Kid could stand up and half holler, "Now wait a minute, Greasy."

Steering his horse careful over to the tracks where he'd have a clear run along the ties, Greasy says, "Long as we're close to town, might's well lay in some good grub. Won't take but a minute," and he galloped off.

The Kid turned on me, angry. "You can't give him no twenty dollars if you expect to see him again inside a week," he says. "He'll have a whole bottle down before I can catch him."

"I didn't have nothing smaller," I says.

"Rich boy," the Kid says. "When you going to pay me for that race you lost?"

"Pay you what?" I says. "I didn't hear no money mentioned."

"You must not of been listening," the Kid says. "What's the use of racing for nothing? I never race for less than five dollars."

"Where's your five dollars?" I says.

"Is it okay if I eat something now?" Fred says. "There wasn't no supper because it was all burnt."

The Kid's face turned red. "I don't happen to have five dollars at the moment," he says.

"You mean you go and make bets when you ain't got the money?" I says. "I may seem like a greenhorn, but I know what they call folks that do that."

The Kid started saddling his horse, not looking at me. "I had it then, but I spent it," he says.

And I could tell he was embarrassed and wished he hadn't said nothing but was mad and worried about Greasy, so I says, "Well, maybe we better start all over again and have another race."

"Any time you say," he says, sounding relieved.

Fred was trickling a little coffee into Greasy's cup, but the pot quit halfway, and he says, "Jackson, I'm empty."

"Well, so am I," I says.

"I ain't used to starting off the day empty," he says. "Not sure I can do it."

"Them Baptist ladies is probably turning flapjacks right now," I says. "Go on and get your share."

"I can't help it if I'm a growing boy," he says.

The Kid bumped his forehead against his saddle, laughing.

"Goldang it," I says to Fred. "Do I have to pay you a dollar a day too? Pretty soon I'll have the whole town hired, then there won't be nothing happening natural except maybe to horses and dogs and fleas which don't know nothing about wages yet. Why don't somebody hire *me* for a change? Where's *my* dollar a day?"

"What're you good for?" the Kid says.

"Horses and dogs get hungry too," Fred says, hanging his head.

"Greasy'll be back," I says, not liking either of them subjects too much, and I set down by the fire to wait.

Fred come over and set down too and looked into the half a cup, sloshing it around, and he says, "I'll split it with you."

"Drink her down, boy," I says, and durned if he didn't do it, not even leaving a drop.

The Kid started off for town but hadn't been gone but three or four minutes—which Fred took up describing the particular kind of gnawing hunger he was feeling, just in case I might of happened to mistake it for some other kind like the gripes—when Greasy come leading the way back with a pair of gunny sacks slung over his horse's rear and the Kid tagging along, looking sheepish. And by the time the Kid had made another pot of coffee, pounding the beans on a flat rock, with me and Fred working the water tank again but not getting dowsed so much, Greasy had laid open a big can of tomatoes, which I hadn't seen the likes of except in a pile of empties back of the hotel, and some hard white biscuits, and had speared four long chunks of bacon and spitted them over the fire.

"Is this how cowpokes start off the day?" I says.

"Well, if you want the whole truth," Greasy says with a big smile showing through his beard, "I'd have to boil some beans and use sowbelly instead of bacon and make the coffee in a dirty frying pan, but at this here big expensive college I'm running, the rich boys have got to get their regular squares if they're going to play ride-the-horsie all day. We can afford a little celebration."

Fred was going at it with both hands, and I pitched in too so's I wouldn't wind up runt of the litter, and when the Kid filled his own cup and give it to me and Fred to share, things seemed friendlier. Greasy half filled up his own and took it over to the far side of his horse and pretended to be lashing his bedroll on tighter, but I heard the clinking when he dug into a gunny sack. In a minute he come back with a full cup, and he says in a big happy voice, "Well, what's it going to be, boys? I been everywhere and I done everything. I been on all sides of cattle, including inside once when old Maggie Lawson give a party in the slaughterhouse, and there ain't nothing I don't know about them stupid devils. I been up in the mountains and out in the desert. I been near drowned and near froze and near roasted. I been cut and shot and jailed and let loose and give up for dead and hung once by mistake and once apurpose. I seen bears bigger'n moose and moose bigger'n locomotives and mosquitoes that could of et them both. I been up so high I couldn't hear myself whistle and it took three hours to boil a pan of water, and I been down so low I had to climb a stump to tie my shoes. I panned more gold than your maws have silverware and been cheated out of more money than I ever seen. I been drunk in every state and territory west of the Mississippi and sober in half of them. I treated dancing girls like ladies and ladies like poison and whiskey like mother's milk. I can see in the dark, talk sign language, spit further than ere a man I ever met, shoot, hunt, track, fish, sing, wrassle, and I'm going to learn how to fly one of these days. I been where the water flows uphill, and I been on the other side to catch it coming down again. I seen the earth shake and I seen it hold still, and between the two for drinking purposes I'll take her holding still. If there's some place else to go and something else to do, I'll go there and do it, long as it don't violate my principles which is if a man takes anything, he's got to put part back, and do your washing downstream and your drinking upstream. Life is short and full of blisters, boys, so where do you want to start?" His cup was empty by the time he finished, and he give it a sad look.

"Why don't we start off hitting the trail?" the Kid says. "Sun'll be up."

"Don't go rushing my pupils here," Greasy says.

The Kid says, "One of my principles is when you listen to old men talk, you got to put half of it back where it come from."

Greasy got another half a cup poured before the Kid could start dumping it out with the grounds, and then he stretched and paced around a little like he was loosening up his legs, zigzagging toward his horse nice and casual, looking all around at the mist and the bushes like they was interesting sights, till he could get at the gunny sacks again, so to cover up a little for him, I says, "What we need first is learning how to ride without getting kilt."

"That's right," Fred says with his mouth crammed full of biscuits. "Though I didn't fall off but oncet yet."

"Well," Greasy says, clinking away at a sack, "that'll take some thought."

"While he's thinking, go rench these out," the Kid says, handing me the coffeepot with two spoons in it—and the two tin plates—so I drug Fred with me, still chewing, and we clumb up to the spout again and come back half wet.

"That'll take some thought," Greasy says in a loud voice, holding both elbows way out to drink his coffee and working his face and his jaw and his eyebrows after he swallowed. "Kick some sand on that fire, Kid."

"Kick it yourself," the Kid says. "I ain't one of your pupils."

"The first thing to learn about riding is your horse," Greasy says, tilting his hat back and frowning and pacing back and forth slow. "And the first thing a horse wants to find out is when do we eat, and after he finds that out, he wants to know what *you* want so's he can do something different. That's where the hard part comes in. Some things a horse wants to do, you want him to do anyway, so you just let him, but it's them other things that cause all the trouble."

"You mean like if he wants to go south and you want to go north?" Fred says.

"Now there's four ways a horse can tell what you're thinking," Greasy says, blowing and sipping his coffee. "Through your legs, through your rear end, through your hands, and through your voice. There's a fifth way, but you can't help how you smell till you learn the other ways and quit being scairt."

The Kid was kicking out the fire and tying up his bedroll, so I started doing whatever he was doing and Fred followed suit.

"A horse that's got any sense knows just exactly what the butt of a coward feels like, just like you might know one looking him in the eye," Greasy says.

Rubbing the seat of my pants, I says, "If my horse can feel anything through there, she's doing better'n me."

"A horse is better'n you at *most* things, son," Greasy says.

"Even an old jackknifed billygoat that looks like a leaky flour sack like what's-his-name got there is smarter'n you think. Only trouble is, how you going to find *out* what he knows? *He* ain't going to tell you unless you know how to ask him."

Fred had got his saddle on pretty straight and was trying to fix the cinches, stooping under his horse's belly which hung low, and he says, "How do I ask him?"

"You'll find out later on, boy," Greasy says.

Fred come out from under and looked his horse close in the eye and says, "How you doing, Buster?" And Buster shifted his hind legs back and forth a couple times, lifted his tail, and commenced dropping horse apples.

"Well, that's a good sign," Greasy says. "Time to worry's when the grass quits going through."

I got my saddle heaved up on top of the saddle blanket, and it was the newest and biggest and rawest-looking one of the bunch. I wondered whether I'd ever see it broke in or even use it enough to get it dirty, because truth to tell I wasn't feeling a whole lot like a cowboy but more like a kid running away from home—except there wasn't no home.

"And another thing," Greasy says, "if you got any choice, you're better off on the horse than off it, so if you're on, stay on even if he gets to bucking and running, because no matter where you're headed, it beats walking." He tested Fred's and my cinches. "Go on, mount up."

We done so, and he shortened up the stirrups on both of us and says, "If you can't figure out how to take some of the weight off your butts, you're too dumb for college."

Which left me red in the face, and when Greasy went over to his own horse, Fred whispers, "How do you do it?" just like he used to do to me about the Bible and I used to do to him about The Law.

"Sort of stand up a little if it gets rough," I says, that being the only way I could think of except laying down sideways across the saddle on my belly.

"Go on, Kid," Greasy says. "You been voted the most hardworking, eager, good-natured, sober Saturday bullwhacker in this here outfit, so you can be trail boss for a while."

"You know the way better'n I do," the Kid says, kind of sullen.

"If you take a wrong turn, I'll tell you," Greasy says.

I could see the Kid wanted to stay behind Greasy and watch the gunny sacks and maybe keep us from getting too friendly, but he didn't want to say so. He give a twitch of the reins, and the little pinto went skipping up the path out of the sandy hollow by the tracks. Mrs. Sippi started going by herself again, though I didn't let on, and Greasy hung back to shoo at Buster to get him going, and then we was really off, really on the trail.

We couldn't see the town because of the morning mist, but the sun was pouring gold through it now and rolling that misty gold past us toward the west where we was headed over the prairie all notched up with dry crick beds and little clumps of brush. And every step my horse took now was like a step through a gate, one right after another, gate after gate into some new kind of place each time, every one fresh and different and new-made, so's not even the clay and stones and broke little sticks of bushes was the same kind, but getting better. There wasn't one touch of wind. I felt like I was dreaming, which I mean I didn't reckon on nothing bad happening like in some dreams, monsters and such or people I knew out to whack me up for dinner, but the good kind of dream where you ain't hunting for something or some place you lost, but are in it. The sun kept washing around from behind us like *it* was what kept us moving, and then I commenced to cry.

Part of me was real surprised and didn't know what all that water was doing interfering with the view, but the rest of me knew what it was and just let it rip. I didn't make no noise doing it and kept my head and shoulders straight-front so Fred and Greasy wouldn't see, and I was finished with it before the Kid ever turned around to look.

18

———— • ————

"Now this here is foxtail grass," Greasy says, taking a clump in one hand and shaking it around and stretching one leg at a time. We was all trying to stand in the shade of the one little old tree which somehow or other hadn't got chopped down for firewood over the years, though it had plenty of whacks in its bent trunk and looked about to die. "See how the horses ain't too interested?"

They were nibbling at it a little, and Mrs. Sippi had one strand stuck in her teeth like a jayhawker come to town to see the sights, but they weren't chomping it much.

"Same with bronco grass and squirreltail grass," Greasy says. "I'll show you some when we come to it. They'll eat it and so'll cattle, but it don't do them much good. What they need is bunch grass or buffalo grass which has got green blood in it."

The land was a little rollier now, and it seemed like you could see further than you really could—for instance, the Big Horn Mountains ahead of us was clearer than ever, gray and lavender and raw-looking like they'd been scratched open—but I hadn't even seen the tree we was standing under till I was near close enough to hit it with a rock. It was getting to be Injun country where you could hide out in the open in little dips and draws and gullies that only come up to your knees. And the sun was up high and hard.

"You figure you could get us a job at this ranch?" I says.

"Well, I don't know," Greasy says, scratching his beard.

"Job doing what?" the Kid says. "Swamping out the bunk-house?"

"Everybody's got to learn sometime," I says.

"Who says you got to learn?" the Kid says. "Why don't you go on learn something else you're fit for?"

"Well, we was going to be lawyers," Fred says, "but I reckon we'll have to wait now till we make some money."

Laughing, the Kid says, "Ever seen a rich cowboy?"

"Now don't go changing the subject," Greasy says. "How'm I supposed to fill up these pair of sheepskins here if all you want to talk about is jobs and money and all that trash? These boys got the right idea: first you learn something, then you figure out what good it is."

Greasy's breath was like it just come out of a snifter, and it made me kind of dizzy there in that skinny little bit of shade, but I liked listening to him. "All right, what's next?" I says.

"What's next is we're going to pretend like we got two thousand head of cattle with us," Greasy says, "and you're going to learn every dang job on a trail crew."

"Well, I'll be a lousy buffalo-skinning bowlegged son of a cracker if I ever heard the like of this," the Kid says. "We're never going to get there on time, you old chunk of bearbait. Now leave off all this fool stuff, and let's go."

"There ain't but eleven men on a crew and only seven jobs, and three of *them's* alike," Greasy says, "so it won't take long. Now, let's see."

He strolled over to his horse and just kind of slid up onto it without thinking, and he seemed too strong for an old man. We all went out in the sunshine and mounted up.

"First, there's trail bossing which is what it sounds like," Greasy says. "He leads the way and says stop or go and can hire and fire and settle arguments, but most important he's got to find water because cattle can dry up in a hurry in this crazy kind of country." He licked his lips and glanced at the Kid. "Go on, Kid, show them how to find water."

The Kid scowled, hesitated, then pinched his lips together and started trotting off. "Make it fast," he says.

Greasy watched him go, then fumbled a half-full bottle out of one gunny sack, uncorked it, and took a quick jolt. Looking a little guilty, he says, "Talking's thirsty work, and a little choke-dog never hurt nobody."

The Kid was a couple hundred yards off now, dipping in and out of sight and heading toward the mountains, and our horses started walking along after.

"Now how do you find water?" Greasy says.

"Go hunt up a crick?" Fred says.

"How do you find a crick if you don't know where it's at?" Greasy says.

Fred shrugged and looked at me, and I says, "Go downhill?"

"Which way's downhill from here?" Greasy says.

And of course there wasn't no such a thing where we was,

just little dips and dry washes. "I don't know," I says. "The way the Kid's going?"

"Which way's the Kid going?" Greasy says.

"Toward the mountains," Fred says, beating me to it.

"If you was up in the mountains, you'd know which way was downhill, wouldn't you?" Greasy says.

"I hope so," I says.

"If you couldn't do it no other way, you could fall down and see which way you rolled," Greasy says. "Now if a mountain's got any size to it at all, it's going to have a crick, maybe even a river. Look for color at the foot and go for green. That's what he's doing."

"He's been this way before, though," I says, not wanting the Kid to be too good at it.

"Or trees," Fred says. "If there ain't any mountains, look for trees."

"That's right," Greasy says, looking surprised. "You learn what cottonwood, willow, and aspen looks like, even if you can only see one little tip of it sticking out a mile away, and you're on the right trail. Or pretty soon you learn to smell water, and if you can't, your horse can. Just let it get its nose out of the dust a minute, and it'll find you some water."

"When do we eat?" Fred says.

"Ask the trail boss," Greasy says, but the Kid wasn't even in sight.

"Eleven men got to handle two thousand cattle?" I says, not liking the odds. "What do you reckon they do in their spare time?"

"Well, one's the cook and one's the horse wrangler," Greasy says, "but them's no-account jobs that an old lady could do if she felt like it—and the night herder if you want to count him, which is even more low-down than the wrangler: drives the bed wagon and spells off the wrangler till maybe four o'clock in the morning. But you get yourself a job on left or right point—that's up front—and you get to be a roper and a cut-out man, and you're somebody." He was dead serious like a preacher ranking angels. "Course, you don't get to ride point for nothing. You got to come up from drag—they're eating dust way in the back—to flank and then to swing. Got to work your way up, and maybe it can take years, and some don't never make it."

"Does it pay good?" Fred says.

Greasy chucked at his horse to speed her up a little, and Mrs. Sippi give a surge forward and started bouncing under me, and I seen Fred's hands go out with no reins in them like somebody walking across a plank, but he didn't fall off.

"You don't do this for money," Greasy says, sounding like he was in pain.

"What's the main idea of it all?" I says between bumps.

"You seen dogs punching sheep, ain't you?" Greasy says. "Same thing except cattle ain't quite so sheepish."

"Does a cook have to ride a horse?" Fred says, his voice jogging.

"Not unless somebody's chasing him," Greasy says.

"Maybe I should practice up cooking," Fred says.

Greasy ignored him. "Let's pretend like I'm riding left point, just moseying along, waiting for the trail boss to show up on the horizon some place—" and just as he was saying it, there come the Kid way off to the right on a little rise, and stuck his hand up in the air three times, then took off his hat and swung it around. "There's our water about three miles straight past where the Kid is, so what do I do?"

"I think something's getting broke in my butt," Fred says.

I wouldn't of said that for another shammy bag full of twenty-dollar pieces, but it sure felt good to hear *some*body say it.

"I'll tell you what I do," Greasy says. "I start crowding my side of the point and getting a little ahead of it." He begun speeding up some more. "And what does the feller do over on right point?"

I had to clench my teeth to get the words out steady enough to sound like words, and I stiffened my knees a little. "He slacks off some," I says.

"That's right," Greasy says. "By God, we'll get these here cattle to water yet." He clicked his tongue, and his horse went into a canter, pulling away from me and Fred and kicking up enough dust to give me an idea what a whole herd of beef could do.

And then Fred started hollering *Whoa* at his horse, which I could of told him didn't do no good but the opposite, and as a matter of fact I *did* tell him. I says, "Shut up! Don't yell!"

But he was saying, "Whoa! Whoa!" louder and louder and closer and closer together and pulling back on the reins, which didn't do much good neither because his horse commenced rearing and twisting and trying to climb a tree that wasn't there.

I seen Greasy take another slug out of his bottle, and it was a good thing he'd already lost most of his front teeth because he'd of had to lose them all over again then and there. He'd gone off way ahead of us now, curving to the right, but when Fred started whoaing again louder than ever, Greasy turned and come galloping back at us, which Mrs. Sippi didn't seem to like none.

"Hush up or you'll get the whole shebang turning too far," Greasy shouts. "You'll stampede 'em."

I tried to tell him it wasn't me doing nothing, but Fred getting panicky because his butt hurt, but just then Mrs. Sippi woke up and turned herself half inside out and headed southeast right through the middle of where all the cattle was supposed to be, and she went loping steady and fast just like she done in town.

"Jumping Jehoshaphat!" Greasy yells at me, which didn't give me a whole lot of information what I was supposed to do, and Mrs. Sippi seemed to get broader and longer as she went, spraddling my legs out almost flat, and I don't think it would of made no difference to her if the cattle *had* been there: she'd of split them two thousand in half and clomped right over the stragglers and not thought nothing about it because she had her mind made up again. I could almost see it working through the back of her big thick chestnut-colored hairy skull: she had woke up to the pleasures of cutting across country, minding everybody else's business and having none of her own, and it was more like she was riding me than me her.

I remembered what Greasy said about staying on your horse no matter what, but it didn't seem to make no sense to me now, with my bones getting all shook inside me like nails in a can, but I guess I'm stubborn after all (which he says a cowboy has got to be, even if it's dumb-stubborn), so I stuck with her, trying not to whack the saddle too hard every time she jolted stiff-legged at the ground and took another giant step which seemed like twenty yards a try. In one way she made it easy for me because I didn't have to do no thinking, mainly because I wasn't doing nothing apurpose, nothing voluntary, but in another way, doing nothing on her back was the hardest work I ever got stuck with. And now she was all perked up with her ears aimed forward and her nose straight out, shifting a little from side to side like she was scouting for something to do.

And she found it when we come to a little rise with a wedge-shaped wash behind it and there stood a milky-colored scruffy-looking bull calf about two-thirds grown with grass hanging out of its mouth, staring at us like we was the biggest surprise since thunder, and naturally it swung around and started running the way they do—faster than you think they can, though I'd never seen one do it from up on horseback before but setting down on the boardwalk or leaning on a fence—and Mrs. Sippi acted like a dog just seen a cat. She went into a hard gallop and come out on the level again side by side with the calf like I didn't have nothing better to do than clang on to her neck with both arms and get myself beat to death with my own saddle.

The wind had laid the brim of my sombrero down flat over my eyes, and I couldn't see much except out the corners, but I seen more'n I wanted to: the ground was going under us so fast I couldn't even tell what she was running on, but it sounded hard and I didn't want to land on it. And there was the calf going higgledy-split next to me, trying to curve away all the time, but Mrs. Sippi kept in tight, and I'd lost the stirrups long ago, and them small black pointy horns was bobbing and jouncing right below. Then we seemed to hit a patch of rougher ground, and it was just like a light surrey trying to go too fast over stones in a creek bed, and before I knew what was what, I'd skidded off her and flopped onto the calf but too far forward to ride it. All I could do was hang onto everything I could reach and keep my head between the horns, and I felt my legs get thrown off the calf's back and start dragging, and I just let them drag, not having much choice, and felt myself getting pulled around under it, but I didn't let go because I didn't want to hit the ground going that fast. And all of a sudden the calf put on the brakes and ducked its head and dipped and laid down hard on my legs and just stayed there probably because I wouldn't let go of its head: I didn't want them horns on the loose, and besides one of them was hooked under my old man's belt buckle and, if I let it up too soon, I might not touch ground till the next county because my old man's belts was built to last.

Mrs. Sippi had stopped too and come back to give me a sniff-over, not even breathing hard though I could see a little lather on her chest, and the calf just laid there, trying to keep the grass in its belly I expect. I heard another horse come pounding up and stop.

"If that ain't the dangedest thing I ever see," Greasy says. "Who learned you how to do that?"

"I don't know," I says. "Get me up."

"I wasn't going to learn you how to do that for a month or two," Greasy says. "How'm I supposed to earn my dollar a day if you do everything on your own hook?"

"Right now I got my pants hooked," I says.

When he come around where I could see him, he was off his horse and had a short length of rope which he used to lash a fore and hind leg together with. Then he eased the horn away from dangerous territory and heaved up the calf's rump so's I could haul out my legs, and I was glad to see the toes of my boots still pointing frontwards. Then I had time to give Mrs. Sippi a dirty look, but it didn't seem to bother her none. "I think my horse must of belonged to a cow-puncher," I says.

"I do believe you may be right," Greasy says. "See how she's standing with her front legs braced? She ain't sure but what you lassooed that slit ear and left the other end tied to her."

I didn't want to think about Mrs. Sippi for a while, so I nursed myself back to health by watching the Kid round up Fred out near the horizon and start aiming him at us, and when I looked back at Greasy he was picking up an armload of brush which he brung back and dropped. "I believe I heard you say you could start a fire, Junior."

"You ain't going to eat that calf, are you?" I says.

He laughed and begun rummaging in his big saddlebags, and at first I thought it was going to be time for another drink, but instead he pulled out a chunk of twisted-up black iron. "I ain't so dumb as to eat my own cattle before they're full grown and had a chance to take a long drink before they got on the scales," he says. He fished around in the heap of brush and come up with a stick to jam into a slot in the iron. Then he held it out at me so's I could see, and there was three big black X's.

"How do you know that calf's yours?" I says.

"Well, he's going to have my brand on him in about fifteen minutes, ain't he?" Greasy says.

I looked all around every which way in case some rancher might have his boys out after us. "Is that rustling?" I says.

"It's just an old Western custom, Junior," he says, motioning at the brush for me to get started. "Mavericks on the open range belong to the man that gets his mark on there first, long as he ain't known to be dishonest." He looked me in the eye without blinking or smiling. "Or long as he ain't too unpopular with the people who got most of the cattle in the neighborhood."

He watched while I started making a bunch of tepees inside each other out of the brush and sticks, and when I didn't say nothing, he says, "Or long as he got any kind of money and could of bought it some place."

When I finished, he handed me a sulfur match, and I stayed knelt down and lit it and fed the fire up, having to blow on it now and then.

"It ain't exactly illegal," he says, going for a gunny sack and hauling out the bottle for a quick one before the Kid got in range.

The calf was just laying there quiet like I wished I could of done because I was sore all over, and I says, "Funny, I don't recollect selling this here maverick to you."

There was a long quiet spell. Then Greasy says, "How's that, Junior?"

"I caught this calf with my own bare hands," I says. "How's come it don't belong to me?"

"I roped its legs, didn't I?" Greasy says.

"I'm much obliged to you," I says. "How much does a piece of rope that size cost? I'll be glad to buy it from you since I don't happen to have none of my own, and we might run into some more mavericks."

"All right, all right," he says. "You're just like your old man, standing on the letter of the law except when it don't happen to be convenient. What you fixing to brand it with, your teeth?"

I held my shirt back from my belt buckle with the big AJH-LLD gleaming in the sunshine, and I says, "There'd ought to be some way to use this, I reckon." I looked at the calf again, kind of worried. "Will it hurt?"

Sounding disgusted, Greasy says, "Well, I don't guess it'll hurt much, long as you take it off first."

I fanned the fire with my hat, and he commenced doing the same on the other side, blowing ashes in my face. I could tell he was kind of mad at me, and come right down to it, I didn't have much idea how to put a brand on any calf, even if it was tied down. But it was too late now, so I took off the belt, which wasn't doing no good anyway because my jeans was so tight, and looked it over. The leather had been looped back at one end and riveted to hold the buckle on. "How hot does it have to be?" I says.

"You better let the calf figure that out, Junior," Greasy says, getting up and stretching and going back to lean on his knapsack.

I tossed on some more sticks, wishing I hadn't started rounding up no cattle, and I says, "Maybe it don't need a brand. I reckon I'll remember what it looks like without no letters on it."

"If you don't do it, that maverick's going to have a nice big triple X on him like a keg of whiskey, boy," Greasy says.

I stood up for a minute and watched Fred fall off his horse —or maybe it was just the way he decided to climb off—and him and the Kid begun to have a little conversation with Fred laying on the ground.

"Can I borry your knife?" I says.

"Why, sure," Greasy says, pulling a little sheath knife off his hip. "That's another way to do it, but you got to be careful not to cut too deep or it won't heal right and you might croak him."

I took the knife and cut a slit alongside the rivet and finally squeezed the loop open and had the buckle free. Fred was standing up now but not going near his horse, and the Kid was jawing at him from up on the pinto, still holding the other reins. I give the knife back, dropped the buckle in the fire, and tried to shove the sticks in close with my boot, but the fire didn't look hot enough to boil water on even, so I fanned it some more. "Was you ever in my old man's courtroom?" I says.

"Three times, far as I recollect," Greasy says.

"Did he jail you?" I says, hoping not.

"Son, I was in jail before he ever laid eyes on me," Greasy says. "He just made it official."

"What was it for?"

"Now, son, you don't want to go asking a man a thing like that," Greasy says, taking a pull on the bottle and watching the Kid get off his pinto and shove Fred toward the other horse. "But it wasn't for killing and it wasn't for stealing nothing."

Fred took a swing and knocked the Kid flat on his back,

and the pinto bolted off sideways, going strong, and by the time the Kid got up and scrambled onto Fred's horse and started after it, it was halfway toward that water I'd been hearing about.

"The Kid ain't mean," Greasy says. "He's just a mother hen and he don't know when to duck, neither, but don't mess with him if it's guns. He can shoot almost as good as me."

Fred begun trudging toward us, and I says, "Reckon I'll ever be good at anything?"

"You already are," Greasy says, laughing a little and watching the Kid disappear over a shallow rise after his horse. "You got enough gall for a whole gang of young'uns."

"What's gall good for besides making stones?" I says, remembering MacIsaac's old lady who died with a mess of them.

"Well, I guess that's what you come to find out," he says.

I fanned the fire some more and blew on it and after a couple minutes, when Fred was coming close, I give the milky buff flank of the calf a good look over, trying to locate some place where it wouldn't hurt much.

"Now you take the Kid," Greasy says. "Smart as he is, he didn't remember to let his reins trail when he was off his horse. You can be good at something and still do it terrible sometimes."

I got the last couple of spare sticks, each about a foot long, and stood looking at that belt buckle which was in the hottest part of the fire but didn't seem to be turning red. "I don't suppose you'd like to do this instead of me," I says.

"No, I thank you kindly," Greasy says.

Trying to use the sticks like a pair of pinchers, I got aholt of the buckle, and they started smoking and sparking and got me all flustered so's I dropped the buckle low on the calf's ribs where it stuck on, singeing away, but the critter jerked and begun bawling, and I seen the buckle was going to fall off, so I clamped my boot sole on to keep it in place and bore down to hold the critter too, and for a second the smoke slid out around it, and then I done some jerking and yelling myself and had to hop and skip a couple times till my foot cooled off.

That maverick had a brand-new H-LL on its side, though it didn't look very deep, and I had a backwards J like a fish-hook on my boot sole.

"Well, I guess one of you owns the other now," Greasy says, "but I'd hate to say which was which's."

"Which way's home from here?" Fred says, limping into range.

But I didn't even bother to answer a fool question like that.

19

———— • ————

By late afternoon, with Fred walking, we'd made it over to the water the Kid had located which turned out to be a crick the size of a hall carpet with some bushes and bent-over willows clumped along it here and there, and we made camp again, a little more careful this time, but there wasn't no sand to lay on. I'd brung my calf along on a rope I'd had to buy off Greasy, though they'd all tried to talk me out of it. I couldn't see no sense in turning it loose if it was mine.

"What you going to do when you get yourself a couple hundred head?" Greasy says, lounging back against his saddle and taking a good pull at his special Red Eye coffee. "You going to leash them all up like a pack of hound dogs?" He got a laugh out of the idea.

So did the Kid, who was all dusty and mad from chasing

around. "I'd like to be there when they take a notion to go three ways at oncet," the Kid says.

"When I get a couple hundred head, I'm going to do the same thing you done when you had two thousand," I says. "I'm going to ride point."

"Well, you better let them cattle know what you're doing ahead of time," Greasy says. "Trouble with cattle, they can't tell what some people is doing. They might make a mistake and think you was a trick rider excaped from Buffalo Bill's Wild West Show and get all lined up to watch instead of herding off some place."

Fred was laying face down near the fire, poking a couple sticks in now and then, and even though the sun was still up, it was running out of yellow and going red and purple, and a chill was creeping down out of the hills in the west. We was too close to the hills to see the mountains now.

"What's the best way to walk from here?" Fred says, making his voice sound strong and businesslike.

"Depends on where you want to get to," the Kid says, opening another big can of tomatoes with a hunting knife.

Greasy chuckled along at that and took another pull on his coffee cup. "Well, I'll tell you what you do," he says.

"Because I can't ride no horse," Fred says. "I'd sooner go barefoot and blindfold through stickers."

"Tell you what," Greasy says. "This here crick empties into the Powder and that empties into the Yellowstone and that empties into the Missouri, so if you feel like swimming, you can get most anywheres you want to between here and New Orleans."

"That's a good idea," Fred says, looking back at the water. "I could make me a raft and get off some place near Chicago and catch the train to Harvard."

"Sure," Greasy says. "Why don't you and the Cattle Baron here float yourself a herd of cattle along too. Keep you company. They might even do pretty good in that Harvard too, about as good as you're doing here."

"I'm still paying a dollar a day," I says. My butt was sore too, but I wasn't quitting.

"All right, all right, I'm giving my good advice, ain't I?" Greasy says. "It's coming up for Saturday night and we're home on the range, but I ain't complaining. Go ahead. What do you want to know? Cowboy College is still in session, it ain't never been out of it."

"I hope that booze is all going to be gone before we get to the ranch," the Kid says.

"I'm doing my best to get it all down, ain't I?" Greasy says.

Something was stirring in the back of my mind, and I says, "Suppose you wanted to find somebody that had lit out ahead of you. Suppose you wanted to follow his trail even if it was a couple days old. How would you do it?"

"Well, there's all kind of ways to track," Greasy says. "Depends on who you're tracking, whether he's smart or dumb or careful or in a hurry or whether he knows you're after him and what kind of country you're in and what season it is, and all like that."

"Take it like here and now," I says. "Suppose somebody's been through here ahead of us."

"I don't have to suppose nothing," Greasy says. "They *have* been."

"Who, where?" I says.

"Right along the crick here," he says. "Two horses and some kind of little wagon."

"Only they wasn't both pulling the wagon," the Kid says.

"That's right," Greasy says, yawning and getting his back settled in against his saddlebags. "Two days ago, maybe a little less."

"How'd you know all that?" I says.

"Oh, Land of Goshen, boy," Greasy says, sounding tired. "Go on over by our horses."

I got up and went over where we'd staked them after they'd been good and watered and stood there listening to them munch off the low brush.

"Go on around to the rear ends," Greasy says, and I done so. "Now look down on the ground."

I looked.

"What do you see?" he says.

"Horse apples," I says, feeling like he was joking with me, especially when the Kid begun chuckling.

"All right," Greasy says. "They're brand-fresh, new-made right out of the oven. Feel a couple of them."

I touched some of Mrs. Sippi's with the toe of my boot.

"I said feel a couple," Greasy says. "With your fingers."

I stood and looked at him for a while, and the Kid went on chuckling and Fred perked up and quit staring at the water. "I don't think I feel like doing that," I says.

"You only have to do it oncet," Greasy says. "Then on, you can tell by just looking." He waited a few more seconds, and when I didn't do nothing, he says, "You want me to learn you something or don't you?"

"Yes," I says, still not doing it.

"Well, you got a crick right there beside you to wash your lily-white hands in, ain't you?" he says.

"Yes," I says, still not feeling like it, but then I stooped over and done it quick.

"No, no," Greasy says. "You got to pinch one till it cracks open."

So while I was at it, I stooped again and done what he said.

"Now, are your fingers wet, damp, or dry?" Greasy says.

"I guess damp," I says, heading for the crick to rench them off.

"That means it's getting on for a couple hours old," Greasy says. "Of course, if it's real hot summertime you got to make allowances."

He still sounded serious and practical, so I didn't mind the Kid chuckling.

"Now go on down where that little willow bush got broke off in the water," Greasy says.

Swiping my hand back and forth to dry it off, I says, "How's come you're not out here learning this too, Fred?" I didn't like the way he was grinning.

"You go on learn this part and I'll learn something else," Fred says. "Don't need but one horse-apple man. Besides, I ain't tracking nobody."

I went where Greasy told me, and he says, "What do you see?"

"More," I says.

"Does it look the same?"

"No, it looks old," I says.

"How'd you take that notion?" Greasy says. "Is it growing gray hair on it or something?"

"It's dark and dry-looking," I says.

"Go on, pinch one of them," Greasy says, and I done so before I could change my mind.

"When do we eat?" Fred says.

"Shut up and learn something," Greasy says. "Now what's the difference?"

"It ain't quite dried up," I says. "But almost."

"By tomorrow it will be," Greasy says. "Now you been shaking hands with one of the genuine gold-filled 21-jewel screw-case timepieces of the prairie, Junior, and you ain't never going to forget it."

I washed my hand again and then stood looking at the four narrow grooves left by front and back wagonwheels that come within a couple feet of the crick and wondering whether it was my old man's surrey done it, and if so, what difference it'd make. "What was somebody doing way out here in a surrey?" I says.

"It could of been a surrey," Greasy says, not sounding too interested.

And if it was, I might of pitched the very hay and chucked the very oats that went to make them horse apples, which at the moment didn't give me no sense of achievement but a hollow feeling.

"You can all come and eat this mess now," the Kid says. "But starting tomorrow, we got a new cook."

"We're going to learn Frederick the Grunt here how to rustle beans," Greasy says.

"I didn't figure on being no cook," Fred says.

"What else you good for?" the Kid says.

Fred shut his mouth and looked like he was trying to think, and I brung back an armload of sticks for the fire because the dark was pulling in close now and the air was going chilly with it.

20

—— • ——

After we'd et, I handed Greasy the cigar that Brady give me
what seemed like two months ago but was two days, and it
was pretty near two cigars by now, having got bent and
shredded some in the middle. But Greasy liked it fine, wet-
ting it up in his coffee and rolling it back together and set-
ting fire to it. He offered me and Fred some eating tobacco,
but we'd already got sick on that last summer, so we shied
off.

"Now this here wouldn't be a bad bed ground for a herd
of cattle," Greasy says. "Matter of fact, we ain't far off the
Bozeman Trail, so it's probably been used for just that. We'd
all of us be taking two-hour turns at night guard, keeping
our little Herefords from getting the nightmares."

I strolled off a ways to have a look at my bull calf which

I'd tied to a strong bush out past the horses. I'd used a good stretch of rope so's he'd have eating room, but he'd went and shortened it by winding around and through the bush so he barely had enough left to get facing me when I come close. He didn't exactly want to run away and he didn't want to charge neither, he didn't know what he wanted to do except he didn't have enough room to do it, so he just stood there with a wet nose and stared at me. He wasn't no Hereford but he might of been partly—the white curls was beginning to sprout up between his half-growed horns—and I was as bad off as he was: I wanted to turn him loose and I wanted to keep him with me, right up next to the fire with a blanket on him, and I wanted to leave him tied up right where he was. Putting that shallow brand on him hadn't changed nothing: Greasy'd brushed half of it off with his hand and said it wouldn't last through next week and I'd might's well paint my name on it with rhubarb juice. But I didn't care. I'd never had a chance to own nothing like a calf before, and I was glad he hadn't been made into a steer yet so's I could raise him a bull. I looked at him till it was most dark, and he done likewise.

When I come back to the fire, Fred was already rolled up in his blankets and the Kid was laying down on his back with his hands under his head, scowling up at the sky where the stars was coming out thick, and Greasy was onto another bottle, still using his coffee cup but leaving out the coffee now.

"Ordinarily you wouldn't want to sleep this close to a crick because you can't hear nothing proper," Greasy says. "With all that water running, you can't hear what the cattle're doing, and somebody could come up and run off your horses and you wouldn't even know enough to roll over."

I slid into my bedroll, trying to keep warm, and I says, "Are we going to get there tomorrow?"

"Well, we'll come pretty close," Greasy says. "One of the troubles sleeping on the trail is you got your goldanged ear to the ground all the time, and you can't help hearing a jack rabbit stub his toe a mile off."

He give me room to say something, but I was looking at the sky and wondering how's come it never seemed that big before, never so deep and chock full of things.

"You get so you can reckonize all kind of thuds and thumps and scuttering and sounds you didn't pay no attention to before," Greasy says. "I'd learn you how to tell the difference between a horse and a steer, but we'd have to get somebody to go off a ways and run them a little. How about it, Kid?"

"Go to blazes," the Kid says, sounding sleepy.

"Just earning my wages here," Greasy says. "I'd do it myself only I got to be here and tell Junior which is which."

The Kid didn't say nothing, and I says, "I'll learn it some other time." My head was so full of stuff to remember, I didn't think hoofbeats could fit in anyway.

"It's a good idea to learn some stars too," Greasy says, settling back and using his coffee cup to shield the faint firelight out of his eyes. "Never can tell when you might lose track of camp in the dark. You ought to know the North Star—Pole Ass, they call it. All you got to do is find the Dipper and just let your eye go pouring out along the front end of it, and there you are at old Pole Ass. You see?"

He was pointing off some place, but my eyes were blinking off and on and getting blurry. "Yes," I says, but it weren't so.

"Then there's all kind of other stars too," he says, chatting away, and the Kid rolled under his blankets and Fred let out half a snore. "There's Beetle Juice and Old Iron and Canopy and Boots and Aunt Harris and all kind of stars. But you just learn the Dipper and Pole Ass and you'll be all right."

I felt like I was going to be all right whether I learned any more or not. "There sure is an awful lot of territory out here," I says. "I used to think down to the depot and back was a long ways."

"Son, there's more wide-open spaces than there is things to put in them," Greasy says. "There's places so empty you got to keep talking to yourself to keep from getting lost. There's places you could pour in that whole town of yours, and it'd take you a week to find any of it."

I believed him. I'd begun to feel how big the country was and how hard it was going to be to spoil it with all that jangle and jumble about money. There wasn't no trace of a jail or a casino or a bank or a church or a courthouse or nothing else out here, and that was fine with me. Then murmuring from far away a little like the crick, I heard a voice that sounded like Fred saying, "Now I lay me down to sleep. I pray the Lord my soul to keep. If I should die before I wake, I pray the Lord my soul to take," which could of been pretty embarrassing if he'd been awake to hear himself do it.

But the funny thing was, I couldn't be sure he done it because the Kid didn't laugh, and Greasy went right on talking like he hadn't heard nothing, and he says, "Now, what you want to do is bring the whole herd to water with the right point leading, kind of bring them in at an angle so every time another steer gets to the water, he's upstream of the last one. That way they all get clear water before the mud's riled up."

Which sounded logical, and I begun to hear them do it. I must of had my ear to the ground like Greasy said because I could hear a whole lot of deep thumping, slow and steady, and I pictured them all drinking their fill at once and taking the crick right down to a puddle.

"Do you solemnly swear to tell the truth, the whole truth,

and nothing but the truth, so help you God?" my old man says, least it sounded like him, though I knew that couldn't be right.

Greasy kept talking too, but the night started drinking up his words as fast as he could get them out, and it swallered up the crick and the cattle and my old man, and then it swallered me too.

21

———— • ————

In the morning it turned out me and Fred had both kept our souls, but he hadn't done too good in other departments because after we'd all saddled our horses, him too, he wouldn't get on his. He was standing there chewing the last of the beans which he'd been showed how to soak and boil with a little soda (and it had still took two hours). "I can't ride no horse," Fred says.

"Well, if you don't ride it now, you're going to have to eat it in a couple days," the Kid says. "Which would you ruther?"

"Come on," Greasy says. "It ain't but ten miles to Sideslip, and the ranch is only a hoot and holler past that."

"What's that Sideslip?" I says.

"It's a little crossroads that thinks it's going to be a town one of these days," Greasy says. "Big-city boy like you wouldn't hardly notice it."

"I could walk ten miles if I didn't have new boots on," Fred says like he expected his old shoes to fall out of the sky.

"Saddle that bone bag, there, what's-your-name," Greasy says to Fred. "I'm not going to let no kid dry-gulch himself while I'm around. You saddle it and get up there just like you was going to Sunday School or I'll kick the living Jesus H. Christ out of you."

Fred rubbed his hind end. "I can't help it if my back's broke," he says.

"It ain't broke yet," Greasy says. "Not till I get through with it."

"Well, it's going to be your fault," Fred says, climbing up and sort of standing in the stirrups like he was trying to see over a hump and not letting nothing touch the saddle.

Greasy nudged Fred's horse with his toe, and we all started off, me with my calf strung out behind on twenty foot of rope, and the Kid says, "Ain't you going to turn that maverick loose? It's going to spook my horse."

"That horse of yours was born spooky," I says. "But if you're worried, you can saddle up the calf, and I'll lead the pony instead."

The Kid didn't answer, and we all went trotting along through a high fair clear morning, gradually getting the chill of the night jolted out of our bones (least I was), and after one tug on the rope which got the maverick started, Mrs. Sippi kept drifting back and sideways toward him till they was flank by flank and I had to take up some of the slack to keep them both from tripping. The trouble was, Mrs. Sippi wanted to get right up next to him and a little bit ahead and sort of herd him and turn him, and the maverick kept shying off, just like he was supposed to, and we commenced going in a great big clockwise circle, and it didn't matter what I done with the reins: I could of cut them up for shoelaces for all Mrs. Sippi cared.

The rest of them stopped to watch, and when we come around full circle after a bit, I says, "Got any suggestions?"

"Turn it loose," the Kid says.

But I knew that wouldn't do no good. It wasn't the rope but Mrs. Sippi was keeping them two together, so I just stuck with it while she went jouncing out in a big circle again.

When we come around close to the others the second time, Greasy says, "She thinks you want to bulldog it."

But I wasn't aiming to fall off like yesterday. I was hanging on to everything I reckoned was permanent enough to do me any good. And then finally Mrs. Sippi must of caught sight of the rope out of the corner of her eye—or else I was keeping it hauled in too tight and she felt the pressure—because all of a sudden she planted herself solid, and the rope went singing out of my hands till I had enough sense to let go of it altogether, and the maverick went on running out to the end of it to where it was snubbed onto my saddle horn, then done two-thirds of a back flip, landed on his hind legs, and come around facing us, stiff-legged. Mrs. Sippi was backing up now, hauling the maverick a little at the end of the taut rope, and I kept from getting jerked out of the saddle somehow.

"Well, I suppose you can back her into Sideslip," Greasy says. "But we ain't got time to watch the show."

"This ain't my idea," I says.

"Come on," Fred says. "I can't stand up all day."

The Kid rode around behind the maverick, though I could tell the pinto didn't like it none, and started whooshing with his hat and chiyukking, but he scairt the pinto more'n anything else, so he pulled out a small sheath knife and tried to reach the rope.

"There's no call for that," Greasy says. "That's *my* rope."

But the Kid went right on slashing, and if the pinto hadn't been so restless—doing skids and hoppity-skips every which way—he'd of cut it in no time. But just then the maverick took a notion to make another run for it. And because Mrs. Sippi was holding still, backing off, keeping the rope stiff, and always facing the maverick, there wasn't no place for him to run but around in a circle, which he done. And he hadn't even made one whole turn before the rope caught up with the pinto which tried to skip it like a girl playing jump rope, but it was too high and scraped up over the pinto's rump, as the maverick kept running, and took the Kid right out of the saddle and set him down hard on the ground, and then because Fred's horse come wandering in close to Mrs. Sippi like it wanted to see what was going on, the rope started coming right at it (moving slower than out near the maverick) and Fred's horse ducked a little and went under it, but Fred couldn't do nothing but catch aholt of the rope with both hands and, because it was too low to scrape under and too high to climb over, he had to just let it take him right on off the rear end and onto the ground where he had enough sense to let go.

Looking mad, Greasy come in close to me, plucked the rope off my saddle horn, took a short gallop after the maverick, shortening up on the rope as he went, then stopped his horse cold and give the maverick another lesson at turning inside out.

The pinto commenced running off, and the Kid scrambled up on Fred's horse and lit out after it, cussing, and Fred rolled over onto his knees. "I don't mind falling off," he says like he wanted to explain it logical to himself. "I don't mind. It's getting back on I can't stand."

Mrs. Sippi trotted over to the maverick like she wanted to mother it some more, but Greasy kept his horse in between, and in ten minutes the Kid come back riding the pinto and leading Fred's tuckered-out horse, and he says to me, "I'll get even with you for that, Junior."

"There's a lesson in there," Greasy says, "but I can't figure out what it is." He started his horse at a walk, not taking no nonsense from the maverick which went along tame as a dog. "I never seen such a bunch for biting the dust."

"I ain't fell off lately," I says.

"I expect you'll figure out some way to do it," Greasy says, and the whole procession of us got started, me next to last with Mrs. Sippi snuffing up the pinto and Fred leading his horse at first and limping on foot, but after about five minutes, he'd clumb up on the saddle and was laying over it on his belly like a drunk cowpoke getting sent back where he come from, which I had thought of before he did. And his horse followed right along without getting aimed, and I had come to believe that was the way most horseback riding got done.

He rode like that all the way to Sideslip which we come to in the late afternoon. It was a little clump of shacks and a half a dozen stores alongside a crick with a patch or two of water in it, and we come to a road when we was still about a half mile outside and we could see how it run into the town and then branched west and north. "Now we can let somebody else do the cooking," Greasy says, smacking his lips, but since he hadn't been drinking nothing so far that day, I reckoned he might be thinking about refilling his gunny sacks.

I'd never been in another town before, and I was glad to

be starting out small. This one didn't look like it had made up its mind yet whether it was coming or going, and there wasn't hardly any junk laying around on the outskirts and only a few wagons clomping along, yet after a couple days out in the open, I felt kind of crowded the closer we come to it, and when we made it as far as the first tin cans and shacks, it seemed like I should get off my horse and walk, but even Fred was staying on, so I did too.

And there up ahead on the main corner with a cluster of people around like at a medicine show was a one-horse phaeton with two big people in it, a man dressed in Sunday black and a woman wearing one of them garden-patch hats with a couple of blue birdwings sticking up out of it. They each was holding up a pair of open champagne bottles and taking swigs now and then, and I could hear them both jawing at the same time, loud and happy, even before I reckonized them as Rev. Haskell and Lulu. There was a couple empty bottles on the ground, so they must of been working at it a while already.

We all stopped to listen, and Fred scrambled up the right way on his saddle and sat there gawping, and when Lulu paused to take a longer drink than usual, we could hear Rev. Haskell saying, "And this church will not be held in the confines of manmade walls, and your prayers will not sail up and bounce off of manmade rafters on their way to the living God, but they will rise in the open air like birds on the wing and fulfill their mission at the speed of thought."

"How much you selling that stuff for?" some wiseacre in a flat hat says up front.

"This ain't for sale no more than God's love," Rev. Haskell says, taking a pull out of one of his bottles. "In this church every man will be called upon to bring his own vessel of communion and—"

Lulu come chiming in twicet as loud, "And there's going

to be two kind of vessels of communion to reach your hearts without no shame and no remorse, because women has been took advantage of too long." She was slurring a little, and her mouth looked to be coming open more on one side than the other. "The female body, nekkid as it was made, will carry your souls to Heaven here on earth. The way to the heights is through the fallen, and I know where to get the very finest and cleanest fallen women there is, and if that don't do the trick—"

Rev. Haskell says, "Before the wine of our days is flat and sour, leave us quaff it to the full openly in the eyes of the Lord Jesus Christ who said to Mary Magdalene who had been a whore for years and years, 'Come with me and sin no more,' and by God she come."

"It's only sinning if you sell it," Lulu hollers. "So I'm giving it away."

"Well, give me a bottle and I'll see what I can do," another wiseacre says.

Rev. Haskell's eyes was so wide open it didn't seem like he could move them without he moved his whole head, so he hadn't seen Fred yet. "I can show you all a wonderful light after the years of darkness," he says. "The house of the Lord must burn to the ground before it's fit to live in, and a man must burn in sin before he's fit to house the Lord." He took a quick swig, trying to start talking again before Lulu could barge in, but she was too fast for him.

"And a woman can be your bed of coals," she says. "Just lay down and burn on her."

"There's no use sitting indoors on a Sunday, praying for salvation on the resurrected blood of the Savior," Rev. Haskell yells. "You got to resurrect your *own* blood, you got to make it rise and shine, you got to get out of the dark pews and parlors and sinful vestries, come out under the sky and rejoice!"

"Hallelujah!" the first wiseacre says.

"Ladies' Night in the Turkish Bath!" the second one says.

"The female form should not stay wrapped up and hidden from the light of day," Lulu hollers, trying to stand up in the phaeton but crunching her hat up under the canopy. She kept herself from tipping over by hanging onto the case of champagne on the seat between them. She had on some kind of a thick dark cape that come down as far as her waist and was tied around her neck with a bow, and she was trying to slip the bow without letting go of either of the bottles.

Greasy looked at Fred and me to see what we was thinking, then worked his horse in a little closer to the phaeton, dragging my maverick with him.

" 'I will bless the Lord at all times,' " Rev. Haskell yells. " 'His praise shall continually be in my mouth,' " he says, getting the neck of the bottle in there as quick as he could and taking a pull.

"There ain't no wickedness if there ain't no shame," Lulu says, sounding half strangled because she was bunching her neck in and yanking on the ribbon at the same time. "So if you want to run the wickedness out of your town, all you got to do is quit shaming people." She give up on the ribbon and tried to sling the cape back over both shoulders, giving herself a good douse of champagne down the back of the neck.

"Lulu, if you're going to spill that stuff, you might's well spill a little on me," Greasy says.

"I got christened a new name which happens to be Mary Magdalene Morehouse," she says, "so anybody wants to address me got to use the right name."

"That's right," the first wiseacre says. "I heard they hit them battleships a lick with a bottle to get them started."

"Well, Maggie, my dear," Greasy says, "it's been a long dry day so far, and I'd be pleased to drink your health." He half took a bottle away from her and she half give it to him, and he commenced drinking it down.

Squinting, she says, "Is that you, Greasy?"

He nodded and smiled around the bottle neck but didn't interrupt himself to say nothing, and Rev. Haskell says, "Behold, I show you a great mystery, which men shall be like little children, and little children shall be like men, and women shall be like mice, and money shall be like the pebbles on the pathway into the wilderness, and horses and dogs shall weep for the corruption of the dead, and there shall be nothing for supper but wine and bread bought and paid for by the lusts of men."

"What you doing in Sideslip?" Mary Magdalene Morehouse says.

"I guess I'm slipping," Greasy says when he could get the bottle out of his mouth.

"Me too," she says, but then her voice raised up while she dug another bottle out of the case, and she yells, "My husband and me are foundering the First Church of Bread and Wine." And she come up with a loaf of bread too, having to tuck it under her arm a minute while she tore the wrappings off the new bottle.

"Hey, Pa," Fred says, sounding worried.

"We're going to make our church right here on the corner," Rev. Haskell says, "out in the open where nothing can catch fire but souls."

"The hell you say," a bald man in a butcher's apron says, standing over by the general store ten feet away. "You can't go blocking my entrance."

"Hey, Pa," Fred says louder.

The kids and wiseacres gawked around at him and seen him looking at Rev. Haskell, and one of them says, "Is that your pa?"

"We'll make you a new entrance here to a new life, so don't you worry none," Mary Magdalene Morehouse says, popping the champagne cork past Rev. Haskell's ear and causing the Kid's pinto to back halfway out in the street. "We're going to call it the First Church of the Second Honeymoon."

"We already called it something else," Rev. Haskell says, frowning.

"You go to your church, and I'll go to mine," she says.

Handing back the empty, Greasy says, "How do I join up?" and he held out his hand like he expected another bottle, but she didn't give it to him.

She spread her arms like she was going to make a speech, but Rev. Haskell pointed past her straight at Fred and says, "You're no son of mine."

"How come?" Fred says. "I didn't do nothing."

"My name's the Rev. Oxymoron Morehouse, changed legal and aboveboard, and I got divorce papers," Fred's old man says, fumbling through his inside coat pockets. "Papers in both names to prove it, so go on home."

"You went and burned it down," Fred says.

"You leave my husband alone, young man," Mary Magdalene says, sticking herself between them and rocking the phaeton. "He's got enough on his mind without looking backwards."

Rev. Morehouse pulled out a bunch of legal-looking papers which must of set old Shanklin back a couple hours but was probably worth it to get rid of them both. "We're going to have a burning ceremony," he says.

Snatching them out of his hands, Mary Magdalene says, "Don't! That's our wedding papers and divorce papers and all that." She commenced stuffing them down her bosom where there wasn't enough room to mail a postcard.

"We got to burn the church mortgage," Rev. Morehouse says.

She spread her big arms again, spilling papers and champagne, and she says, "You see before you a pore downtrodden product of lust, hard liquor, and hard luck. Once I was pure as the morning dew, but that dew wound up in a shot glass and was drank down straight by the Son of the Night. And now I'm being made pure again, and I'm about to fall on the fields of morning."

"You're about to fall on your head," the first wiseacre says.

"Shut your hole," Greasy says to him.

"Take a good look," Mary Magdalene says, wrenching at her neck ribbon again and breaking it finally so's her cape crumpled down on the seat. "Underneath this bosom beats the purest heart in the West." She cradled both bottles against it. "No babe has ever suckled here."

"Nor wanted to," the second wiseacre says.

"Besides, babes ain't no good at waiting in line," the first wiseacre says.

"I told you to shut your hole," Greasy says, scowling down at them.

"And who might you be, old-timer?" the first wiseacre says.

"I'm the man that's telling you to act polite in front of a lady," Greasy says.

"You put one up there, and I'll do it," the first wiseacre says.

Raising her voice, Mary Magdalene says, "But many a year a she-wolf's been carrying that pure heart around who might do any blame thing she pleases." She heisted her skirts for a second and kicked the first wiseacre in the face without looking at him, and he went over backwards among the kids. "I'm nettles and bobwire, I'm quicklime and liniment, I'm pumice and buckshot. Whenever I get up, the sun goes down—if it knows what's good for it. I got a rattle in my tail that lights up in the dark, I eat little boys and clean my teeth with their pizzles, I know where the Lost Cabin Mine is, and I don't give a durn for the Governor or the President or the King of the Mountain. I'm wild and woolly and full of fleas, and they curry me with a hay rake, and the man ain't been born yet can keep me down on my back." The wiseacre made a grab at her leg, and she took a pause to kick him in the face again.

Rev. Morehouse, getting red from keeping quiet so long, spread out his arms too, and the whole phaeton seemed plumb full and overflowing with them. He says, "And now, my dear friends—"

"What's all this here about now?" a little squat man in a white Stetson says, pushing his way through and showing a badge on his vest. "You can't go throwing bottles around here and raising a rumpus."

"Hi, Mort," Greasy says.

"This ain't Saturday night, it's Sunday," Mort says, not sounding sure and final and steady the way a sheriff ought, but sort of apologetic. "Hi, Greasy."

"These folks is on their honeymoon," Greasy says.

"Well, why don't they go over to the boardinghouse and do it proper?" Mort says.

"I can scrape the clouds out of the sky a month at a time," Rev. Morehouse says, like he was applying for a job, but the people didn't look like the kind that wants to hire anybody, least not for money, and there wasn't no women except one peeking out of the store. "I can heal the lame, the halt, and the blind as long as it isn't something permanent."

"What's wrong with you, Archie?" Mort says.

And the first wiseacre honks some of the blood out of his nose and says, "She kicked me."

"Now, Mort, it didn't amount to nothing," Greasy says.

"Assault and battery," the first wiseacre says.

"She don't run on a battery, she runs on steam," Greasy says, looking worried and getting off his horse, having to shoo some kids away to make room. He glanced around and handed me the rope to the maverick.

"I think you all better clear out of here now," Mort says, but not sounding too firm about it. "You too," he says to Mary Magdalene.

"Us two what?" she says. "I can make it rain or snow or hail or sleet or sunshine. I can make frogs fall out of the sky, I can butcher hogs with my bare hands, and I can call snakes from a mile off." She begun unsnapping her dress in the back.

"I can call 'em too, but they don't come," the second wiseacre says.

"It's about time to calm down, lady," Mort says, turning on the kids and lunkheads and hollering, "Clear off!"

"I can see into the future," Rev. Morehouse says.

"So can I," she says, peeling her dress down and showing her huge white shoulders and lungs bulging out of the top of a frilly pale-green corset big enough to lay out for a hammock. "I ain't never going to be shamed again. Who's going to cast the first stone? Let's have it right now."

I seen a lunkhead picking up a small rock on the other side of the street, but before I could do anything, Mort had shoved up next to the phaeton and was trying to haul her dress back up, but he was too short to reach far enough.

She batted his hands away and says, "I'm going to be nekkid before my Lord!"

"Now, now, Mary Magdalene," Rev. Morehouse says. "I can wait."

"You ain't my Lord," she says. "You're just a communion vessel like me."

"I'm going to ask you to halt in the name of the law," Mort says, trying to toss her dress up and hook it on her lungs, but it kept sliding down.

She give him a half kick in the chest, which was pretty polite considering what she done to the wiseacre, but Mort didn't like it. He staggered back and pulled out his sixgun, and just like magic it seemed like the street was clear except for me and Fred and the Kid and Greasy.

But she didn't pay no attention and begun unstringing the laces of her corset, keeping aholt of one bottle of champagne, which slowed her down some.

"I'll have to ask you to come along with me now, folks," Mort says, meaning the Rev. and Mrs. Morehouse and waving his gun at them.

Greasy took it away from him, just plucked it away and broke it open and dumped the bullets out in his own hand and give it back, and he says, "Mort, I don't like to see nobody pointed at, it ain't polite to point. I'll clear them out of town myself without no trouble."

"You can't do that to me," Mort says.

"I already done it, so talk sense," Greasy says, getting around between Mort and the phaeton.

Pulling a couple of bullets out of his belt, Mort tried to stick them in the cylinder, but Greasy took the gun away again and says, "Now just leave off."

Rev. Morehouse sat down and shook his head like somebody'd dropped a collection plate in the middle of his prayer, and Mary Magdalene says, "I won't have nobody fighting over me. There's plenty to go around, boys."

From across the street, peeking around the edge of the corner store, the first wiseacre hollers, "Put your dress back on, honey, you're making everybody sick."

"You can't talk to my wife like that," Rev. Morehouse says,

falling out the other side of the phaeton and sliding down off the wheel and catching at it till he was kneeling in the dirt.

Greasy put his arm around Mort and begun talking in his ear, strolling him along a few steps and nudging him friendly and keeping the gun just out of reach, and Fred clumb down off his horse to help his old man who didn't seem to want no help.

"Ezekiel saw the wheel," Rev. Morehouse says, hanging on to it with his eyes closed.

Letting most of the air out of her mouth—and wherever else she kept it—Mary Magdalene set down hard, rocking the boat, and laid halfway back like she was going to rest for a minute.

Greasy was still sweet-talking Mort and even doing some listening now and then, and the townsfolk was beginning to come out from under cover, and the Kid says, "We got to get moving."

Making a shush motion at him, Greasy kept listening to Mort who pointed up at a two-story building next to the grocery, then held out his hand till Greasy nodded and put the gun in it.

"We *got* to go," the Kid says. "We got to muster in by sundown or—" and he give Greasy a scowl instead of finishing.

"I reckon I better stay," Fred says, standing behind his old man and looking worried.

I watched Greasy tilt up a champagne bottle, and I didn't know what to do. He got up on his horse, not looking too happy about it.

"It's now or never," the Kid says.

"Oh, I don't hardly think it's come down to that," Greasy says. Then he looked me in the eye and winked. "Anybody can show you where the Jumping J Ranch is at, Junior. But I expect you got some business here for a bit, besides helping these here church founders get to bed. Mort tells me your old man's upstairs at the boardinghouse with a busted foot, and you might like to pay your respecks."

And him and the Kid trotted on out of town, leaving me holding the maverick's rope.

22

———— • ————

I wasn't surprised, nor any too pleased neither. Seemed like I'd always been finding what I wasn't hunting for, and by this time I'd sort of begun to not hunt for my old man, so when I seen Greasy go riding off to where cowboys go when they graduate, I come near to following without no more family fuss. And if my old man was really up there (which was a place right next to us looked like it would of fell out in the street a year ago if the grocer hadn't let his sign lap over a couple of feet along the front), he wouldn't be no more in the mood to palaver with me than he'd been the night before last.

"What should I do?" Fred says, meaning with the Rev. and Mrs. Morehouse, but taking the words right out of my head.

"Well, it ain't too hot out," I says. "I expect they'll keep till dinner for leftovers." Mary Magdalene had left her mouth hang open like she was hoping for rain, and a couple flies was circling around, looking interested.

Fred reached up and brushed them away. "I better get them indoors," he says, glancing around at the townsfolk who was commencing to gather around like it might be time for the second show. "It don't look right."

I seen Fred was blushing which showed he was persistent if nothing else, acting like the family name was getting drug in the mud even though the Rev. had publicly crossed the name off and hung out a new one. Fred's like that: he wants things to be nice even if they ain't or look nice even if you can see right through them which must of meant his Christian upbringing had took aholt good and proper.

So I clumb down off Mrs. Sippi and hitched her tight to the rail in front of the boardinghouse, acting like I was sure she'd let me do it. "Wait a minute," I says, and went over and knocked on the open door.

The husky, flabby-looking lady that come to the edge of the doorjamb was already shaking her head and holding her wide flat mouth in tight like she wasn't no stranger to the goings-on outside, but I says, "How much?"—that being a question I have yet to hear left unanswered.

"For them? A dollar a day," she says and starts closing the door like she had just won an argument.

"All right," I says, "but you got to help us do the hauling." Me and Fred might of managed them one at a time, but I didn't want to leave neither of them out on the street for the kids to play with meanwhile.

"Let's see the money," she says.

I had to dig into my shammy bag without taking it out of my pocket, but I didn't do no more than show her a gold piece till I could get change some place, since I wasn't aiming to stand the First Church of Bread and Wine no three-week honeymoon in scenic Sideslip.

But the sight of it got her to moving, and she hollers, "Walt!" back in toward the parlor, and pretty soon a scrawny old man come shuffling out with his suspenders hanging to get the bad news which consisted of the north end of Rev. Morehouse while the lady took aholt of the feet. Meanwhile me and Fred manhandled Mary Magdalene out of the phaeton (with me having to get up in it behind her and try hugging her out of the seat). She was clinging on to a little felt cushion with one hand and a small carpetbag with the other. Her being half awake, there wasn't no way to dislodge them short of a free-for-all, so we just let her hang on and commenced lugging the newlyweds upstairs.

The old man and the landlady went up first, which was a good idea because if me and Fred had taken the lead and let Mary Magdalene slip, she would of cleaned out that staircase like a boulder coming down a gulch.

When we was halfway up, Fred says, "Let's change places, Jackson."

Which I thought at first was just one of them notions Fred takes into his head three or four times a day, but then I seen him standing there a couple steps below me with his arms crooked under Mary Magdalene's knees and most of her sinking down below that and her dress cockeyed and Fred with no place decent to look, and I sympathized but there wasn't no way to humor him without dropping her and starting all over again, so I says, "Just close your eyes, it'll be over before you know it."

We finally made it to the top of the stairs, though I'd of sooner tried bringing Mrs. Sippi up backwards the second time around, and we followed the landlady back along the hall past a couple shut doors and into a small bedroom, having to scrape the bride over the threshold, but even at that doing a better job than the Rev. Morehouse could of done in a month of Sundays.

We got her onto the bed alongside the Rev., and they fit just perfect with no more'n an inch to spare in between and out on the edges, and everything was going to be just fine if neither of them had to roll over.

"You reckon I'd ought to undress them?" Fred says, trying to catch his breath. "That's Pa's good suit."

"You better let them decide," I says.

"That'll be one dollar in advance," the landlady says. "I mean two dollars."

"People ain't supposed to sleep with their clothes on," Fred says, sounding like he was repeating a lesson learnt over his mother's knee.

"Well, you done it two nights in a row," I says, and for some reason that seemed to satisfy him.

"Two dollars, please," the landlady says, helping Walt get his suspenders untangled from the Rev.'s right foot before he pulled him off the bed.

I still didn't feel like parting with a gold piece, so I says, "Where does your old man keep his money?"

"What money?" Fred says.

"You figure he was fixing on passing the plate down on the corner?" I says. "He must have something. Look in his pants pocket."

"I couldn't do that," Fred says, looking horrified.

Meanwhile, through it all, I was thinking about my old man being up here some place and worrying maybe I wasn't going to be able to face up to talking to him, even though I felt like I'd learnt a couple new things lately and could hold up my end of a conversation better'n before.

And when I heard some feet clomping in the hall, I got a sudden fear it was him coming on crutches (how'd he got his foot broke anyway?) to stop all this fool commotion while he was trying to sleep, and I was really kind of relieved when I seen it was only Mauger and Pinkus, each aiming a small-sized revolver around the room and grinning like they meant no harm.

Pinkus had lost his hat some place and looked sunburned, and his hair was strawier than ever, and they both looked dusty.

"I thought you'd never get off the street and give us all a little privacy," Mauger says.

The landlady had her hand on her throat like she was trying to catch her heart on the way up. "Two dollars, please," she says very faint and absent-minded.

Moving in a little closer, Mauger settled his dark stare on me and says, "I got a bone to pick with you, Junior, and I can't decide which bone it's going to be. Maybe a chunk out of your head. Where's our dear old dad? Must be around here some place, or that passed-out pastor wouldn't be riding after him." He glanced up and around like he expected to see my old man stuck to the wallpaper.

"I thought *you* was my dad," I says with a straight face.

"Well, that's just temporary," Mauger says, grinning some more. "That's just on paper."

Pinkus come crowding past and got himself a good place at the foot of the bed where he could view the remains, and he says, "My, my, don't they look natural. Where's the money, Fred?"

"There ain't no money," Fred says, sounding hollow.

"You mean you just ain't had time to look yet," Pinkus says. He give Rev. Morehouse's foot a little shake and says, "Hey, Dad, where's it at?" getting no more answer than he would of got from a wooden Injun. He shook harder and raised his voice. "I'm going through your pockets, Dad, just like a whore at daybreak, and my share of the Checker better be some place."

"This is a respectable house," the landlady says, like she wasn't too sure about it.

"How much do you get for these rooms, lady?" Mauger says.

She opened her mouth twice, then says, "Fifty cents a day."

"Got any empties?"

"One," she says.

Mauger took some change out of his pocket and give it to her and says, "Then go on get in it and shut up, and take him with you," meaning Walt who had his mouth open and didn't seem to be following things too close. "See them to their room, Sammy," and Pinkus waved them out in the hall.

Keeping his eyes tight on me, Mauger says, "You went and run away from home, Junior, leaving me sore bereaved."

"She hit you first, not me," I says.

Mauger jumped, then whispers, "Shut up about that in front of Sammy or I'll skin you." He got his temper straight, then says, "Why don't you tell me where he's at? He's nothing to you, is he? What did he ever do for you? Except run out on you when he knew I was going to spoil his game."

"I don't know where he's at," I says.

Pinkus come back and says, "I locked them in, but there's a window she can holler out of."

"Then go on back and sock her one," Mauger says.

Pretending like he didn't hear, Pinkus begun trying to pry loose Mary Magdalene's fingers from around the carpetbag handle, but finally had to unlatch it with her still hanging on. He dug out a bunch of papers and flipped through them, scowling.

"Them don't belong to you," Fred says.

"Oh, shut up," Pinkus says, leafing through and laying out the papers on Mary Magdalene like she was a desk. "It's bad enough having a dumb brother without being reminded of it all the time." He straightened up. "They're not here, Bent. Old Flint must've cashed him out, but where's the cash?"

"Who's your dumb brother?" Fred says.

Pinkus shook his head and wiped the hair out of his eyes. "I think Dad's oats must've got thinned out a little by the time he got around to you. Or else he just picked a better mare back in Kansas."

Watching me close, Mauger says, "You know, Sammy, I don't think Flint told them after all." He smiled even wider like he was going to enjoy what he had to say, even if nobody else did. Then nice and slow he says, "Me and you's half brothers, Junior, just like Sammy and Fred. Only we got left for bastards."

"Abandoned, neglected, and deprived bastards of two rich and respectable men," Pinkus says in a thin voice.

"Wasn't till we threw in together we started getting some place," Mauger says, showing his dark teeth. "And sure enough our dear old dads was still hanging close together, just like they done when they was dumping their oat bags back in Kansas."

I heard what he was saying, but I hadn't commenced to feel anything yet.

Pinkus scattered the papers on Mary Magdalene with a sideswipe, some of them going all the way up the slope where one of the blue birdwings on her hat had slipped around under her bare chin. Then he squoze his way around the foot of the bed, bumping Fred out of the way, and begun rifling Rev. Morehouse's pockets.

"Stop it!" Fred says.

And I seen he was going to fight, guns or no guns, come hell or hair lotion, unless I cooled him down, so I says, "He's your half brother, Fred, so it's in the family. Half in, anyways."

"I ain't rich," Rev. Morehouse says through clenched teeth, his eyes still shut tight. "It's a snare and a delusion."

Pinkus kept digging away, not coming up with nothing but a soaked wad of sulfur matches and a champagne cork, and Mauger says, "I thought I heard Freddie get disowned down on the street, but maybe my ears was out of tune back behind that pickle barrel."

Flinging the cork away, Pinkus says, "There isn't anything to get disowned *from*. He's lost it or didn't get it."

"Maybe Lulu's got it in her corset," Mauger says.

"Well, go on feel for it then," Pinkus says. "You're closer than I am."

Not looking too anxious to try, Mauger says, "What about *my* old man? What's the use of fooling around with this trash here? He could be getting away with twenty times as much."

Pinkus leaned over the Rev. and hollers, "Think you can burn down my nice church and get away with it? I'll burn *you* down, you old hymn croaker," and he tried to light one of the matches but it wouldn't strike.

Giving Mary Magdalene some halfhearted pokes and squeezes around the gut, Mauger says, "I'd sooner crack a safe for it."

"Ever hear of an old madam didn't have a sock full?" Pinkus says.

"She'll keep, they'll both keep," Mauger says, poking me in the side with his revolver and aiming his chin at the door. "Let's take a look around. I got a feeling the Judge ain't far off. I can smell him."

"That's bacon," Pinkus says, sniffing.

"Same thing, pardner," Mauger says, nudging me out in the hall.

And I wanted to hold them up as long as I could in case Pa was trying to hobble downstairs or get himself good and hid, so I says, "What happened to Flint?"

"Time you grew up, Brother," Mauger says, keeping his voice down now. "What you think happens to bankers? Nothing, that's what. Nothing."

"What do you mean, nothing?" Pinkus says. "I winged him, didn't I?"

"You was aiming at your holy father, and you know it," Mauger says. "You couldn't hit the side of a barrel if you was in it. And that Flint's got himself so papered in with the Mayor and Shanklin and everybody else, Shanklin can't paper him out again. I never seen so many papers."

We was all headed up to the front of the house, me in the lead, and Mauger stopped at the first shut door and kicked it open and stuck his head in, but pulled it out again, frowning.

"Use your head, Bent," Pinkus says. "What would he want to come to a place like this for? He's off a thousand miles some place by now."

"*Your* old man come here, didn't he?" Mauger says.

"My old man hasn't got enough sense to spit downwind," Pinkus says. "Who else could line up the whole Checker and pick Lulu?"

Mauger let out a guffaw, and just as we was getting to the last door toward the front, here come Greasy up the stairs with a champagne bottle in each hand, bumping from the rail to the wall and singing,

> "*Bang it, Lulu, bang it,*
> *Bang it good and strong.*
> *What'll we do for bang it*
> *Now Lulu's dead and gone?*"

—which wasn't going to please the landlady none if she could hear it, it not being a respectable song.

I don't think Mauger knew who it was, and Pinkus was too far back in the shuffle to see good in the dim light (I don't expect he'd heard Greasy sing nothing before anyway), and there wasn't no time to think much. If Mauger was going to think at all, he was going to have to do it in a hurry which I had begun to notice weren't a specialty of his, so I guess he didn't bother thinking. He didn't even bother to get the gun out of sight, but just sort of crowded sideways to move out of Greasy's road.

I was holding still (figuring I might learn something, as my old man had told me, which turned out to be half of a new verse to "Bang it, Lulu" that was all Greasy had time for, but it don't look good wrote down), and as he went by, acting full of cheer and yippety-yip, Greasy clonked Mauger on the side of the head with one of the bottles and kept right on going, having to wade through Fred to get to Pinkus who fired off his gun and broke the other bottle. Greasy took the gun away from him, sort of angry, like a teacher snatching a slingshot from a boy who been *told* not to do that, and then went back and picked up Mauger's which he was half sitting on.

Pinkus froze up against the wall with his hands up, and Fred says, "Don't hurt him, he's my brother."

Which shamed me into crouching down and helping Mauger feel his head, and I was glad to find more grease in his hair than blood and no cave-in but a lump. "Same here," I says. "This one's mine."

"Well, how was I supposed to know?" Greasy says. "Why was they pointing these things at you?"

"I guess it's just one of them family matters," I says.

Acting ashamed of himself, Greasy says, "I just hate to see guns pointing at people. I can't help it, it's a weakness, and I ain't responsible for what I do when I see it. I only come back because I couldn't bear to think of all that champagne going to rot."

My brains felt like they wasn't going any faster'n Mauger's, but they commenced to produce an idea, and I says, "Greasy, you done exactly right, and now I got to ask you another favor. If you got any influence with that Mort, could you get him to ride our brothers out of town? Because if they're turned loose, they're just going to start gunning for us again, I expect."

Pinkus started to say something, but Greasy says, "Shut up till you're spoke to."

And I says, "I'd be willing to pay twenty-dollars transportation."

"For that, Mort'd take 'em all the way back to Slope and tuck 'em into bed and sing 'em a lullaby," Greasy says.

So I used the gold piece I'd already plucked out for the landlady, and Greasy herded our brothers downstairs, and Fred went back to make sure the newlyweds hadn't fell out of bed, and I was left free to have my say with my old man, in case he was really there and not off halfway to Harvard to pick up his honorary Doctor of Laws degree.

23

——— • ———

I couldn't find him right away, him not being in that front
room at all, the way I'd sort of pictured him: sitting propped
up in bed with his foot all padded with white bandages,
holding court. But when I went back along the hall, check-
ing doors, past Fred, past the landlady who was having a
few things to say through the panel which wasn't going to
bring the church ladies over for tea, and back to the very
rear where the floorboards started sagging like the carpen-
ters had ran out of good planks and begun skimping on
nails, I felt just like Mauger said *he* felt: I knew I was get-
ting close, but it wasn't so much smelling as tasting. I could
tell by the taste in my mouth I was going to have to speak
my piece, like the time the schoolmarm made me recite "The

Boy Stood on the Burning Deck" with three front teeth missing.

The only other door was open a couple inches, and when I knocked on it, it swung open a foot and showed me a crumpled bed with nobody under it and a washstand with a basin, but the giveaway was the humpback trunk in the corner with a shawl and a piece of Turkey carpet draped over it—my old man's favorite traveling outfit. So I hung back from the door a little, feeling wary, and I says, "Pa? You in there?"

I heard a small choking sob, lady fashion, from behind the half-open door and nothing else, so I says, "It's Jackson, Pa."

There was some scuffling then, and my old man says, "Come in with your hands up. Slow."

I could of just as easy done the opposite—go back the way I come, fast—but something made me go in, same as it would of made me come down to supper or go out back to fetch some straw. And he was standing in the corner in his best black suit, looking fat and rumpled and dusty and worried. His favorite dove from the Checker was crouching behind him (which was better'n the other way around), his right pants leg was tore open and he was holding that foot off the floor, and he had his little nickel-plated Derringer pointed at me. "Stop right there," he says. "Where's the rest of them?"

As long as my hands was up in the air, I took off my sombrero to the dove a few inches, and says, "I hired the sheriff to take them back to Slope. You can get another good head start in the morning."

"Don't tell me what I can get," he says, his voice shaky. He reached around and used the dove like a crutch to get over to the bed. "What are you doing here? Who told you to come after me?" He sat down on it, still keeping the gun

handy, and swung around to lean against the brass bed-
stead, gritting his teeth against the pain. "How'd you find
me?"

"Just happened to be going the same direction, I guess," I
says, starting to feel bad about having my hands up. "I ain't
after you, Pa. That's Mauger. I'm Jackson."

"Well, if you aren't, you must be the only one," he says.
"Dang that Haskell anyway. I told him not to come this
way."

"And I figured as long as I was passing by, I'd stop and
see if there was anything I could do for you," I says. "And
pay my respecks. Is this my new maw?"

"Never mind who she is," he says, getting red around the
nose.

"I'm sorry you got hurt," I says. "Can I put my hands
down?"

He hesitated, then says, "Well, all right. I cracked some-
thing in my ankle getting out of the surrey, but the Doc's
coming to plaster it up for me. Be as good as new." He was
saying it as much to the dove as to me.

I backed off a ways toward the door. "Drop me a line
sometime care of the Jumping J Ranch when you get your-
self located," I says.

"What the blazes you got to do with the Jumping J?" he
says. "And what are you doing with those crazy clothes
on?"

"I'm going to ride for them," I says. "I hope."

"Hold still right there!" he says, not holding the gun on me
to make me do it, so I done it. "What happened to that fund
I set up for law school?"

The dove was dressed just like the housekeeper for her
wedding—chin-high and floor-deep in dark crinoline—and
she was looking disgusted at me like I was interrupting too
regular. It didn't help my concentration none. "Maybe I'll

get around to it some day," I says. "But I expect I'll leave the family business to Mauger."

"What kind of talk is that?" he says. "You're talking like a fool and a milksop. You can't go working on the Jumping J. You *own* it. Didn't you even read the papers I left with Flint?"

"I don't own nothing," I says. "They skinned me out of it. Took them all day, but they done it."

"You can't let them do that," he says, beginning to boom it out like a decree. "Go on back and fight for it!"

"Why should I fight for it when I don't even know if I'm fit to work on it?" I says, not saying half the things I meant. My old man ain't much of a one for discussions, and you got to make a snatch at subjects as they go galloping by.

"Well, you're no son of mine," he says, scowling at the window shade.

"I'm much obliged to you for giving me all them things," I says. "But you must of did something ass-backwards about it. They've got you declared dead."

His eyes went flicking around while he thought that one over. "They did, eh?" he says. "That's good. Then it's clear sailing, honey," he says to the dove. Then he snapped back, frowning at me. "Where do you get off talking to me like that?"

I took off his belt and hung it on the foot of the bed. "You might need a spare in case the other breaks down," I says. "I appreciate the thought, but it don't fit too good."

"What thought?" he says. "What do you know about my thoughts? What do you know about thinking at all?" He caught himself hollering and glanced apologetic at the dove. "I'm sorry, dear. Just a little argument. He'll be getting along now."

"I hope so," she says, not looking at me.

"I see you're traveling light," I says, nodding at the trunk and wondering what he'd brung along with him, wondering what he'd wanted to keep or save out of sixty-five years' worth. "I wish I could give you a copy of WHAT AN OLD MAN OUGHT TO KNOW, but I guess they don't print nothing like that. There's no money in it."

"Are you giving me lip, boy?" he says, his mouth hanging open in amazement like he used to do when somebody was going to get hornswoggled for contempt of court.

"Nope," I says, tipping my sombrero again and commencing to back out the door. "I guess I ain't giving you nothing."

I left Fred still tending to the sick and poor in spirit and went down to the street to get some air.

24

———— • ————

Mort and the wiseacre that hadn't been kicked was carrying Winchesters across their knees and setting in a wagon ready to go, with my brother and Pinkus mounted up on their horses in front of them, and when I strolled over, Mort touched his hatbrim and says, "Howdy, Mr. Holcomb, they won't be no more trouble. Can't go pulling guns on decent folks. We'll put them back over in their own dang county where they belong."

But for all I knew, he was going to turn them loose a mile away, and I didn't much care. "Good luck," I says to my brother.

"Go to hell," he says, not really meaning it.

"I hope you like being married," I says.

He give me a deep narrow steely look. "It won't take Shanklin long to sign another piece of paper," he says.

"Watch out he don't sign one that says your name's John Smith from New York City," I says, giving him two twenty-dollar gold pieces. "That's for some bills I stuck you with. I'll send the rest when I'm sure I can spare it."

He gaped at them, bit one, then says to Pinkus, "See? What did I tell you?" Then to me, "Where'd you get them?"

"Or come to think of it, I'll trade you my Gent's Utah bicycle for the rest of it and call it quits," I says.

"That old Jesus-shouting, mealy-mouthed, crooked, crank-tailed, slobbering, no-good Pa of mine's getting away with it," Pinkus says. "We can't let him do it, Bent."

Rubbing the bump on the side of his head, my brother says, "You can preach out the back door of the Checker on Sundays."

"How's come our old man run away?" I says, it being one of the questions I hadn't got time to wedge in up at the boardinghouse. "What was he scairt of?"

My brother looked surprised, and he says, "Why, he was scairt of *me*."

"Why?" I says.

"Of me and people talking and having to split up his big old pie," my brother says.

"Is that all?" I says. "How's come he didn't stay and fight?"

"Well, you're just too dumb to understand," my brother says. "It's a good thing you ain't going to be handling none of that money."

"Maybe so," I says. "But I ain't scairt of you. How's come *he* was?"

"You'd ought to be," my brother says, trying to talk mean.

"I wish you the best of luck running the family business," I says. "I'll write and let you know how I'm getting along."

My brother looked at me a long couple of seconds and says, "If you don't beat all." Then he leaned over and whispers, "Why don't you tell me where he's at?"

"I don't know," I says.

He looked at me again, then looked me all over and shook his head and says, "You're probably telling the truth." Then to Pinkus, "He's probably telling the mortal truth."

"He's welcome to it," Pinkus says. "Oh, my old man, goldang him!"

My brother leaned over further toward me and says, "I ain't forgot how you snuck up behind me back home and hit me when I wasn't looking." He glanced quick at Pinkus to make sure he was hearing it wasn't the housekeeper had conked him. "You better stay away from me. You better keep out of town."

Which he didn't really mean but said it because Pinkus was there. "You're welcome to it," I says. "I'm going to make something for my own self."

Mort chucked at his pair of horses and flipped the reins, and they begun prodding my brother and Pinkus up the road. "Got to get moving if we're going to get these sweet little boys back across the line before dark," Mort says.

I stood and watched them go, and not a one of them looked back, not even the horses, so there wasn't nothing to wave at.

Greasy had my maverick snubbed to his own saddle horn again, and champagne bottles was sticking out of his gunny sacks. When I walked over to him, he says, "Well, I suppose I got to get going or the Kid'll have a fit back at the ranch." He let air out of his mouth with a whoosh and shook his head. "Never had much of this here bubbly before. Sure can give you a snootful."

"Ain't you afraid of getting fired?" I says.

"Pretty hard to fire a man that's got two jobs," he says, taking a pull on one of the bottles and swinging up into the saddle at the same time.

I went over to the foot of the boardinghouse stairs and hollered up it for Fred, and after a minute he come down carrying Lulu's cushion and saying over his shoulder, "Yes, ma'am, yes ma'am," at the landlady, who was up at the top acting sort of riled.

Fred come out on the street blinking around and looking dazed, and he says, "Lulu was starting to sober up before I got out of there, and she called me son. I don't look nothing like her, do I?"

"Not much," I says. "Come on, we're going out to the Jumping J and sign on as cowpokes."

"I didn't say nothing about what you'd sign on *as*," Greasy says. "But there's always something to do in fall roundup."

"But you know something funny?" Fred says. "I helped my old man undress partway, and he's got gold coins sewed into the lining of his coat and pants and vest because a couple fell out, and I don't even see how he stood up."

"Well, now you mention it, he wasn't doing too good a job," Greasy says.

"And Lulu give me this to sit on," Fred says, shaking the cushion till it jingled inside. "Feel it."

I felt through the cover and stuffing, and they seemed like the same kind of coins I had in my shammy bag.

"You think she done it apurpose?" Fred says. "Maybe I should take it back."

"Listen here, what's-your-name," Greasy says. "If Lulu give you something, you better take it and spend it and never mention it unless you come to pay her back, or you'll get yourself thumped."

"You think so?" Fred says.

"Now, you don't have nothing to worry about," Greasy

says. "Rafferty is going to sign you both on just as soon's he sees you're sober. It don't matter if you don't know nothing." Then all of a sudden sounding kind of worked up and slurry, he says, "And if that dang Irish cockadoodledoo don't like my brand of liquor, maybe I'll just keep right on going up to the Yukon where they's been rounding up gold instead of dumb animals, so what do you think of that?"

I didn't think nothing of it, not being in a thinking mood. I got up on Mrs. Sippi who was standing there just as calm as you please, staring at the maverick and waiting for some action, and Fred put his cushion on top of his saddle and felt it and finally clumb up and crouched on his knees like some kind of trick rider or like he was going to say his prayers. "I ain't ready to do this," he says. "Maybe I should go to Harvard instead."

"Do that next year," I says.

Greasy started leading the way, tilting up a champagne bottle like a bugle, and Fred's horse and my horse begun walking along behind just like they knew what we wanted them to do, and we headed out west of town to start scraping the green off our horns.